Reiki *and* Crystals

Activating the Power of Fire and Ice

KATHY GLOVER SCOTT M.S.W.

REIKI MASTER TEACHER (ASCENDED)

 FriesenPress

Suite 300 - 990 Fort St
Victoria, BC, V8V 3K2
Canada

www.friesenpress.com

ISBN
978-1-4602-7996-0 (Hardcover)
978-1-4602-7997-7 (Paperback)
978-1-4602-7998-4 (eBook)

1. BODY, MIND & SPIRIT, HEALING, ENERGY (CHI KUNG, REIKI, POLARITY)

Distributed to the trade by The Ingram Book Company

About Reiki

"I believe there exists one Supreme Being ~
The Absolute Infinite ~ a dynamic force
that governs the World and Universe.
It is an unseen Spiritual Power that
vibrates and all other powers fade
into insignificant beside it. So, therefore,
it is absolute! I will call it Reiki…
being a Universe force from the
Great Divine Spirit. It belongs who all who long
to seek and desire the art of healing.

~ Hawayo Takata

About Crystals

Every element in the Universe that
makes up physical matter
was formed in the stars.

~ from *Healing Crystals and Gemstones*

Table of Contents

Reiki and Crystals

Activating the Power of Fire and Ice

Opening the Portal of
the Reiki and
Crystals Frequency

You've just opened the door to brand new knowledge, energy and ability in whichever capacity you work and play with Reiki and Crystals. This program *Reiki and Crystals: Activating the Power of Fire and Ice* will rapidly accelerate your healing abilities and spiritual expansion. Here, you will learn a no-nonsense approach that maximizes the energy of Reiki and Crystals and all Earth energies. This innovative approach is new. No other book or program on Reiki or Crystals brings you this frequency and user-friendly tips, powerful tools, and proven techniques. Encoded in this book is Light energy, and knowledge provided by the Ascended Masters, attuning you while you visit these pages.

You know that once you receive attunement to Reiki, your ability to use, work with and channel other healing modalities changes. Any healing system that you use is stronger and more focused as Reiki fuels it through you. Included in this advancement is the ability to strategically and intentionally use crystals and unlock their limitless potential with Reiki energy. Reiki heals. Reiki strengthens and aligns you more fully with your divinely given and guided soul purposes.

The focus here is to raise your vibration, your knowledge and attune you to activate and infuse crystals, minerals, and stones with Reiki energy. The uniqueness of this program is your energetic activation with the inherent knowledge and healing power of crystals and given the ability to maximize their potential. You'll experience rapid expansion for your own physical, mental, emotional and spiritual healing and evolution – and for those whom you assist. I've been teaching this program for nearly ten years as the Ascended Masters gave me the blessed job to communicate this Reiki and Crystals Frequency. You are not reading this by chance.

There are many guides, manuals, and websites to teach you about crystals and minerals and their specific purposes for energy work. Learning this can be a lifetime of study, and one where the student often doubts their intuitive ability and effectiveness. The material here is designed to maximize your active and dormant talents and abilities, increase your intuition and provide you with the means and ability to get big results even from a little stone.

Upon learning this material and experiencing the light activations embedded in this work, my students report great personal shifts and expansion of abilities. Though everyone has different healing and abilities, you will gain in these areas:

- Greater power in channeling Reiki energy

- Activation of the Reiki and Crystals Frequency within you

- Attunements raising your vibration and your Reiki-Crystals healing ability

- Ability to unleash the power of crystals, stones, and minerals

- Expansion of communication channels with Earth energies

- Mastery of the G.R.A.G. Model to accelerate your abilities and knowledge

- Opening your visual, auditory and sensory abilities to receive information from your Guides and crystals

- Rapid learning of the most powerful and affordable crystals to use today with Reiki

- Developing personal connections with the Top Ten Foundational Crystals of the Reiki and Crystals Frequency

- Developing personal connections with the Top Ten Advanced Crystals of the Reiki and Crystals Frequency

- Tips and tools to choose specific and optimal crystals and stones to use

- Clearing and cleansing techniques for your stones

- Increased intuitive knowing and confidence

- Expansion of ability to live a heart-centered life and access the 'field of all possibility' for yourself and others

- Strengthening of the Third Eye, Crown, and Root Chakras, with greater ability to have your head in the Heavens and feet on the Earth

- Unlocking the inner wisdom of the Earth to maximize healing and expansion

- Channeling for yourself and others with the Reiki and Crystals Frequency

- Learning Energy-testing techniques for your use and with others, including how to choose optimal crystals

- Grid building for healing and manifesting

⊚ Grounding tools while working in new dimensions of higher vibration

Our need and ability to access Earth energies for healing are rapidly expanding. Both Reiki and Crystals are energy forces unto themselves – and together they exponentially grow. Engaging with crystals has many layers and levels. Your abilities will continue to grow as your knowledge base, and confidence does. Working with the Reiki and Crystals Frequency is as limitless as you are!

A Seekers Journey
with Reiki and Crystals

Like many kids, my pockets were often full of rocks. Growing up in prairie-like south-western Ontario, there were not many to choose from, yet the foundation for my passion awakened early. My father worked in a limestone quarry. Living in the far west end of the city of Windsor, known as Ojibway Park, our home was above the salt mines, and from time to time we could feel the blasting in the caverns below.

As with many teaching healers, my childhood had challenges. From this, I learned strength and compassion. One of my elementary school highlights was a class trip about two hours from home. We visited a site called Rock Glen, a riverbed where rocks were plentiful, and you could still find fossils. I vividly recall entering the area and not being able to breathe. I was overwhelmed with the energy and the beauty and filled with joy that I didn't understand. Buying my first marble animal statue has evolved to hundreds of crystals, stones and minerals from around the world.

Moving into adulthood, I began to deny my attraction to rocks and crystals. People in my immediate circle thought my interest in Earth energies to be silly, and I shut myself down.

As a social worker and a new mother, I began to explore a deeper spirituality in my early thirties; Reiki came into my life. It arrived shortly after my husband's sudden transfer from Toronto to London, Ontario. We moved with a three- and a one-year-old to a new life. Little did I know how everything would rapidly change. The first time on a Reiki table, words exploded in my head saying "There it is, there it is."

Even with this profound experience, my skepticism was greater than most of my students today. I clearly had a love-hate relationship through the first two degrees of Reiki and used a lot of energy to deny its ease, power, and my shifting consciousness. Looking back, I knew that I was resisting embracing the 'Reiki Consciousness' in my life, as I knew it would lead to becoming my real self. Reiki was like a benevolent tick that got under my skin and would not let go. Now I realize that my resistance and prove-it-to-me attitude contributed to my calling to teach advanced students and expand the Reiki Consciousness and knowledge.

Meeting the Mitchell-Hedges Skull

> *The key that unlocked the door for my ability to access, hear, use and align others with Crystals and Earth energies arrived the day I met Anna Mitchell-Hedges. She was the caretaker of the formidable Crystal Skull that bears her adopted father's surname.*

Following my family's move to the London, Ontario area in 1994, a series of events occurred setting the stage for this meeting. First, a part-time counseling job in Tillsonburg led me to connect with Janis Wall, my first Reiki teacher. She told me of the Mitchell-Hedges Skull and how anyone could visit with it as Anna kept it at her home in Kitchener, about 30 minutes away.

I resisted visiting Anna and the Mitchell-Hedges Skull for some time, though the need to do so was strong within me. Maybe it was my lack of trust and the need to control, or maybe it was that I instinctually knew that there would be no turning back. Now I can see that it was both.

My defenses finally weakened. It was a crisp November day when I first met with Anna and her crystal companion. Her openness, generosity, and strength of spirit came through immediately. I could feel the energy of the Skull even before seeing it, and wondered how living with it daily for all these years had impacted Anna. She offered me a seat and left me to meditate, asking me not to touch the Skull.

As I was still relatively new to energy work, this meeting was quite profound. The energy emanating from the Skull moved over and through me like waves. In its cloudy, yet clear and dense core, I saw rainbows and dolphins. When I closed my eyes, I started rocking rhythmically. Still being a novice at matters of Spirit, I felt overwhelmed and even anxious, yet unable to leave. I experienced the sense of a profound cosmic transmission and deep peace – both very new to me.

Anna brought in tea, and we spoke for some time. I could see that she delighted in telling stories of her childhood and of her finding the Skull as a teen during an archeological expedition of a Mayan ruin in Belize. There has been much controversy about the Skull, how it came into the possession of the Mitchell-Hedges family, and who is the 'rightful' owner. In the times I spent with Anna, her experience and truth felt real and alive as any I've experienced. My deep sense is that her soul purpose was to uncover the Skull and bring it to our awareness for this time of rapid spiritual expansion.

Through all my work with high vibrational crystals, I've never had the pleasure to meet and work with one whose material, energy and ability to transform matches the Mitchell-Hedges Skull. The closest I've come is with a Star Morph Crystal ball purchased through *Song of Stones* on eBay. This crystal ball is a constant nearby as I write.

Meeting Ann Thomas

About the same time as meeting the Crystal Skull, I was seeking a teacher to provide advanced training before Reiki Master. A friend referred me to Ann Thomas, who lived on a horse farm in our area. It was clear that she was a powerful teacher, but little did I know that she had been working with her Guides for the previous ten years and receiving advanced symbols and attunements for Reiki to the Twenty-First Degree.

A strong and ethereal hand in the middle of my back pushed me forward in studying with her. What followed was a rapid spiritual expansion, immediate immersion in self-healing and new abilities. Concurrently, I taught Reiki, spoke professionally, nurtured two children (one with learning issues), managed a household with a spouse who traveled continually and did not have familial supports in the area. It felt like a weight to me at times, though what we required always showed up. The powers-that-be knew what they were doing! As I completed my studies with Ann Thomas, she was called to live on the other side of Canada on Vancouver Island and my husband was transferred again, this time to Ottawa. Here in Canada's capital city with its naturally strong Earth vibration, the Reiki and Crystal Frequency entered my world.

Being Given the Reiki and Crystal Frequency

During a bitter January cold spell in our Canadian winter, I received a message from my group of Guides, who I refer to as Guidance. They are a group of Ascended Masters and Guides working with and through me. There are a few core members – St. John who helps with writing, and Merlin and Hildegard of Bingen, who you will meet in this book.

I was lovingly informed by my Guides to begin teaching Reiki and Crystals together. This message arrived like a life-changing force, followed by a huge learning curve and shift of consciousness. Up until then, I'd been passionately teaching Reiki for ten years and developed quite a resonance with crystals and Earth energies. During the previous few years, I had been actively using crystals in meditation, healing sessions, and to raise the vibration during classes and attunements.

Creating a class to attune people to the new Reiki and Crystals Frequency both excited and triggered anxiety in me.

The next day, while visiting the quaint Quebec village of Wakefield, I ventured into one of my favorite stores that specializes in home and garden decor. I felt pulled by a tractor-beam of energy to a back corner, where I needed to squeeze between two shelves. On the shelf was one lone book with the title *Healing with Crystal and Chakra Energies*. It was quite a beautiful full-color coffee table-style book and on sale! A loud, long laugh burst from me, causing heads to turn in this quiet store.

That evening, I sat in meditation holding my new book. The outline for the class and how to teach it emerged effortlessly. I felt surrounded, supported and sensing the rightness in embracing the unique power of this class. I was told that "students will experience an activation of their ability to access Earth energies through a process of attunement directed from a higher dimension." It became so clear how a new frequency of healing energy is created when Reiki and Crystals are used together with intention and purpose. Wow!

The very next day, while visiting a local big-box bookstore, I was drawn to the 'remainders section' and found one copy of a beautiful book called *Healing with Crystals and Colour*. An inner knowing stopped me from purchasing it. Upon waking the following morning, there was urgency for me to return to the same store where I found a dozen copies of this little purple-covered book on sale. My Guides spoke to me suggesting I use this book as a text for the class. While calculating the costs of using it as a class text, a clerk appeared and handed me a one-day coupon offering an additional half off all purchases over $50. The Universe made it impossible for me to deny or question any further, so I bought the rest of the stock in the city of Ottawa that day!

By April, my first class was full, and the very divinely-guided materials I created were complete. Sitting on the living-room floor the evening before the first class with all the books I had amassed to build my confidence, I finally got the 'cosmic joke' presented to me in January. The beautiful coffee-table book I had purchased – but not really read – was the same book as the little purple-covered one purchased for the class! It was simply bound and printed in a different format! Thankfully, the two-day class went brilliantly.

Teaching this class for ten years and expanding the program to include the Top Ten Lists of Foundational and Advanced Crystals with Reiki, Chakra Healing Spreads, Grids and Channeling, brings us to the information and exercises presented for you in this book. Know that your experience will be one of intense, deep learning, healing and rapid expansion of your abilities to be in service to others. Enjoy!

Here I am with my new friend at Las Vegas Minerals and Gems.
It is the largest quartz crystal ball in the world!

Part I

Reiki and Crystals:
Twin Flames Together

Reiki and Crystals:
Twin Flames Together

For those of us living Spirit-led lives, we know that relationships are divinely guided. A Soulmate is someone with a similar Soul Contract and Soul Purpose in this lifetime. When Soulmates connect, both experience an increase of energy, life becomes brighter and challenges become easier. A Twin Flame connection is more rare and powerful than with a Soulmate. Twin Flames have a higher purpose directed from Source, with generations of planning to bring two people together. When Twin Flames connect, both of their lives open in a new way, with profound expansion for both of them. Twin Flame connections hold the energetic potential for great relationships, businesses and careers together. The marriage of Reiki and Crystals with the formation of the new frequency given to us now embodies the highest vibration Twin Flame relationship possible. It is a marriage whose benefits are gifted to us for our evolution and healing.

Gratefully, I've been gifted with this new frequency of energy for expansion and healing to share with you. My Guidance continually informs me that my ascended mastery level work on the Earth is a 'bridge.' With Reiki and Crystals, it is a bridge between Ascended Master knowledge and high vibrational expansion and healing energies and the Lightworkers who need this advanced knowledge. The term 'Fire and Ice' refers to this new Reiki and Crystal Frequency. Reiki is the 'Fire' and the word 'Ice' includes crystals, stones, and minerals that carry the consciousness, wisdom and grace of Mother Earth.

Know too that you have chosen to be born now to be part of *the greatest shift* of mass consciousness since humankind began. The combination of these two events has created a portal to healing on this planet for all living beings and the Earth as a whole. Using Reiki energies with the vibration of crystals and other earthly gifts is one of the most powerful healing means available to you today.

Recently a student asked, "What do you mean by Fire and Ice and what makes what you are teaching so different from working with Reiki alone?" Little did she know that to answer this question would take the scope of this book!

> *Your Reiki strengthens and aligns you more fully with your divinely given and guided power. Earth Consciousness waits for you to listen, learn, expand and heal through her. Your ability to access her wisdom is strengthened and aligned whenever Reiki flows without restriction. Reiki activates Earth energies to their fullest potential and increases the intimacy and healing between you and the consciousness of the Earth.*

Shifts in Earth Energies

There have been great openings in the Earth's energies over the past few years. As you may already know, they are part of the master plan for the growth of our planetary consciousness. Sometimes, the outcomes of these shifts are visible and sometimes traumatic. Many of us have been sending energy to assist with the suffering.

Know that the most powerful shifts often herald a new awakening of Earth energies. These shifts bring light and balance to our planet, paving the way for higher frequency energies to ground here. A great example is the arrival of higher frequency children with remarkable abilities since December 2012. This shift also opens up the possibility of healing and transformation with Earth frequencies greater than we have ever known before.

Know that you and all other Lightworkers are feeling and accessing these newly arriving energies for healing and spiritual evolution and in work with others. It is time for you now to bring healing and Light energies to whatever is your work or wherever you may go.

> *The combination of the awakening of new Earth energies, the shift in mass consciousness and your presence here now, enables a portal of healing on this planet for all life and the Earth as a whole.*

Using Reiki energies with the vibration of crystals and Earth energies is one of the most powerful means available to you today to accelerate your healing and soul expansion, to build your skill set and channel a much higher frequency of energy for yourself and others.

Greater Presence of Ascended Masters

Ascended Masters are highly evolved beings each assigned to hold a field of specialized and advanced information and energy. Some of them have lived on Earth, and others have never incarnated in human form. Their time has come to assist us more intimately and provide learning for our evolution and future. With the opening of Fifth Dimensional and crystalline energies on the planet following December 2012, they are in closer contact with you than ever before possible. In a recent meditation, Ascended Master Melchizedek provided the following information to be shared with you here:

> *¡Rapidamente!* is the notice that you are receiving on this day. (Day meaning an extended period of time and meaning right now in this lifetime for you). Do not

hesitate nor get mired in the bog of distraction and false-ness. Be pleased with your being and progress as you carry the pennant for the shifting change and the agents that we are sending to assist. Notice the blessings in your life. Grace is around you and in you now and activates with each step you take on solid ground. Do not waiver! Put one foot in front of the other only on solid ground. We cannot say this enough – solid ground. Do not trust what does not appear as meaningful and etherically tangible. Feel it – listen and think with your heart. Act meaningfully and thoughtfully – using your mind for its intended purpose. Others need your joy and cheer in their life and never minimize the depth of your impact. Most of what happens in the light (of day) has little or no meaning to your evolution. What is done in the dark (at night) is enabling YOU to be who you are intended to be.

Again, this program, *Reiki and Crystals: Activating the Power of Fire and Ice* is different than other crystal healing courses. The uniqueness comes through the activations you receive, through the exercises and healing tools provided in this book. Healing codes are also embedded in these pages that activate new energies and abilities at the deepest levels within you. Right now, you are being aligned with the highest frequency and ability to work with Reiki and Crystal energies. To repeat:

Earth energies and our need to access them for healing are rapidly expanding. Both Reiki and Crystals are energy forces unto themselves – and together they exponentially grow.

What is Reiki?

"My Reiki Ryoho is an original method based on intuitive power in the Universe. By this power, the body gets healthy and enhances happiness of life and peaceful mind."

~ Dr. Usui, from the Usui Reiki Hikkei

Reiki is the Universal Life Force or God consciousness. It is the frequency of love through which joy and miracles flow. The system of Reiki provides us with the conduit to access, receive, manage and make real on the Earth this force for practical use in our daily lives.

We are genetically built to channel the Reiki Frequency. The process of attunement activates dormant DNA and lights this ability in people. Animals and plants can hold the Reiki Frequency as well.

Reiki is an ancient technique for healing and transformation that came back to us through Dr. Mikao Usui. He rediscovered it in this form in the 1920s. Reiki is now a global spiritual and social movement as the result of Dr. Hayashi, Mrs. Takata, and her 22 Master students. Less than 100 years later, it is conservatively estimated that there are 3 million practitioners and over half a million Reiki Masters in the world. Reiki opens the door

REIKI

to the divine matrix of all possibility. Begin to see Reiki as a field of energy that grows stronger each time you draw a symbol, place your hands with healing intention or send Reiki at a distance. Knowing that all change comes through a shift in consciousness, what a powerful force we activate together!

Reiki is the God-consciousness
brought to Earth in a systematic way.

This force activates the chi energy that courses through your physical being and optimally changes you at the cellular level in your body. This is only the beginning of the healing shift and changes that Reiki activates, produces and manifests.

How a person thinks, comprehends and loves shifts dramatically once they invite the God consciousness through Reiki to light the way in their life. Many people 'take' or 'do' Reiki without fully allowing in this consciousness. They only see Reiki as a force, or something separate from self, which keeps Reiki and its transformational nature set apart from their personal essence. You must fully invite Reiki into your life.

Reiki is about change. Upon being attuned to Reiki, most people experience subtle and sometimes dramatic shifts and changes in their lives. Know that these changes are always for the highest good and to allow your Light to shine brighter. All people experience reactions to attunements, as their body cleans and clears old lower frequencies and opens to new energies, becoming the multi-dimensional beings they are meant to be.

Reiki is love made real that activates your true soul self.

You can explain to someone what Reiki is, yet they cannot sense what Reiki is until it is experienced. Often, a person needs to observe and experience the outcomes of Reiki to have proof that it works. Sometimes the results are so subtle and not immediately seen as Reiki healing is a process. My primary teacher, Ann Thomas, wrote the following to describe Mrs. Takata and the evolution of Reiki:

> *"She did not pass on the same process to each of the 22 Masters that she taught. For me, the answer is that as individuals, we have different needs, and there are many paths to wholeness. We each find where we need to be and to learn what we came here for. It is important to honor each other's process whether or not it is the same as our own. Each has an equal value in this journey home."*
>
> *~ Ann Thomas, 1997*

Common Features of All Reiki Schools

Although the methodology of Reiki teachings may vary, several distinct features remain true:

1. Reiki is the God-consciousness brought to Earth in a systematic way. Through the attunement process, you are activated to channel this Source energy for use in a very tangible way.

2. Reiki raises the chi life force in everything that it touches. It enables profound change below the cellular level in all living things for healing on all four bodies – the physical, mental, emotional and spiritual.

3. Reiki is love made real that activates your true soul self.

4. Through healing and focusing your mind (a.k.a. your intention) you can maximize and accelerate the healing, growth and change abilities of Reiki.

5. We are beginning to see how Reiki is a system of healing with both scientific elements *and* consciousness. It comes through us as a force, a wave, and a frequency. As human beings, we are evolving to become better able to work with its quantum nature of all possibility.

6. Reiki is the most powerful frequency for healing and transformation that is available to each and every person on this planet. Reiki is a conduit for living in a State of Grace.

7. Reiki aligns, expands and activates frequencies of energy that people may not traditionally think of as 'being alive.' This face of Reiki enables you to access the consciousness of Mother Earth. Held by her is a mighty force that contains the greatest wisdom available to us on this planet. Man-made power sources pale in comparison to what is readily and joyfully available through her.

The seventh point sums up the previous six and brings us to the limitless possibilities in the Twin Flame marriage of Reiki and Crystals.

> *The God-consciousness channeled through the systematic practice of Reiki enables us as humans to access, comprehend, direct and heal using the most powerful natural method of the God-force on Earth. Crystals, minerals, and gems are tools that represent and hold this consciousness.*

Meditating on the Higher Purpose of Reiki

Here is a beautiful, powerful passage from my primary teacher, Ann Thomas. Read this passage slowly, and then hold your hands over it and meditate. Allow the waves of its meaning to move through you and teach you energetically:

> *The REIKI system of natural healing is a system of symbols. The symbols are the language of the higher dimensions that attune us to a higher frequency. They literally change the vibrational frequency of each cell of our body to help us heal.*
>
> *We are looking forward to a new time, a new age, on Earth when the old way of being will be forgotten as we evolve and see more clearly how to live in a world where the frequency of love predominates, instead of the frequency of separation and fear as in the past.*
>
> *~ Ann Thomas, 1997*

Embracing the Reiki Consciousness

One of the miracles of Reiki is that every living being can have the Reiki light turned on within and access its limitless possibilities for self and others. Consider Reiki a spiritual and social revolution. After 10,000 years with the predominance of masculine energy on our planet, the divine feminine energies are returning to the Earth. Reiki's rise comes at the same time. A coincidence? I think not.

Many people have learned the practice of Reiki. Not all people embrace the 'Reiki Consciousness.' Those who embrace it, learn to let Reiki guide them while flowing through their entire life. Life becomes the experience of living in a State of Grace, attracting what is required and being elevated through the challenging times. Reiki too is the force that attracts and manifests abundance and joy.

Those who have been attuned to Reiki and resist embracing the Reiki Consciousness often fragment Reiki by seeing it as something separate from their full being. They see Reiki as something they do rather than who they are while moving through life. Remaining in this perception negates what Reiki can provide for the self and does not allow its miracle-producing nature to shine. Embracing the Reiki Consciousness is required to unleash the power and wisdom available through working with Reiki and Earth energies, including crystals.

Holding the Reiki Consciousness means you live from your highest self each and every day:

Your highest self is the personification of your soul's aware-
ness of who you are and what you came here to do and
what you are meant to learn.

One of the greatest gifts that Reiki provides to you is the ability to discover and uncover your highest self. When you actively practice Reiki, heal yourself and live from your heart chakra, your highest soul-self reveals more thoroughly. The energy of your highest self is centered between your heart and throat chakras. Know and trust that your highest self is the fully alive potential of who you are and the Light that you are meant to radiate in the world.

Accept that Reiki is an indefinable, intangible, higher-dimensional frequency that your third-dimensional human mind cannot ever fully understand. Know that Reiki is not meant to be understood. It is meant to be trusted, integrated, and activated within and through you for your optimal good, soul awakening, and then for the benefit of others.

Three Methods to Strengthen your Reiki Consciousness

To engage with Reiki and Crystals and their limitless potential for healing and spiritual expansion, embracing the Reiki Consciousness is the key. Following a daily routine or practice helps. The following are three examples of how you can move to action and more fully activate and embrace the Reiki Consciousness in your daily life:

#1 Dr. Usui's Reiki Prayer

One of the simplest ways to strengthen your Reiki is to keep the words of Dr. Usui in your consciousness and vision each and every day. As he said in his prayer, each morning speak these words and during the day have these words available to you wherever you go. You may not always feel connected with the prayer or understand what it means, yet keep it in your awareness and read and repeat the words as often as you can. There is power embedded in the words of this prayer giving you strength and guidance. There are several, slightly differing forms available of Dr. Usui's Prayer. This one is my favorite:

> The secret method of inviting blessings.
> The spiritual medicine of many illnesses.
> For today only anger not, worry not.
> Be grateful and humble
> Do your work with appreciation.
> Be kind to all.
> In the morning and at night,
> with hands held in prayer,
> Think this in your mind; chant this with your mouth.
> The Usui Reiki Method to change your
> mind and body for the better

> ~ Mikao Usui

To build Reiki Consciousness, keep this prayer visible, repeat it through the day. Post it where you feel comfortable, and where you can find it easily. Try your bathroom mirror, the screensaver on your computer or phone, or even as a slip of paper in your pocket. Let your imagination guide you.

#2 Invocation Before Bed

An incredibly powerful manifesting tool is to invoke your Guides to assist and work for you while you are asleep. Say the following before bed each night. Doing this will call on your own Guides and also open you so that the consciousness of Reiki integrates deeply in you.

Write the following words in your handwriting, exactly as given below, as Guidance tells me that this channeled prayer is infused with transformative energies. Repeat aloud or silently three times before bed. Use a tone of excitement and expectancy for the gifts you are to receive:

> *Blessings for the healing, learning, connection and love experienced today.*
>
> *I am grateful for today.*
>
> *I make a request that the Consciousness of Reiki resides more deeply within me.*
>
> *And that all healing and learning I receive continues to be for my highest good and as gently as possible.*
>
> *Help me sleep soundly tonight surrounded by your Golden Light, and awaken rested and grounded in the new tomorrow.*
>
> *~ KGS*

#3 Shifting Your Operating System

To create a solid foundation of Reiki Consciousness in your life, a deep shift in your own 'operating system' is needed. Your operating system is the compilation of your beliefs, commitments, intentions, and level of vibration that propels you forward in the world each day.

Maximizing your operating system and embracing the Reiki Consciousness comes through releasing energetic blockages and core beliefs that keep you fragmented from living Reiki fully. You may not be conscious of these blockages or beliefs, yet when you observe the patterns in your life, you see how they impact your choices both positive and negative. Examples of blockages may include:

- ⑨ Deep-seated perceptions of the validity of energy work

- ⑨ General societal beliefs or those of others in your life regarding Reiki

- ⑨ Your own beliefs about being worthy and deserving of living as a light-filled and powerful human being

Sometimes these blockages have developed in this lifetime or can stem from past-life experiences. Our wisest teachers and healers all had to surrender and work to release core blockages to embrace the Reiki Consciousness and expand spiritually. For me, the memory and awareness of five lifetimes where I was killed or maimed for being a powerful Lightworker required healing and release. The following is an exercise that will help with moving out blockages in your operating system and will strengthen your Reiki Consciousness.

Exercise to Shift Your Operating System

Completing the following exercise will release blockages stopping you from fully living the Reiki Consciousness and having it flow as you move through your life. New channels within you open, deepening the healing that occurs and expanding you and your heart chakra. It also strengthens your Reiki and opens the door to your ability to work and channel with Reiki and Crystals. What you will require:

- ⑨ 13 days with time allotted for meditation and journaling your observations

◎ 20-30 minutes maximum each day

◎ Consecutive days are the best. You can complete this anytime during the day

◎ Use these two Usui Symbols if you have them: Chokurei (Power Symbol) and Hen Sha Ze Shonen (Distance Symbol)

◎ You may or may not want music as an accompaniment

◎ Notebook to record your observations

For 13 days, schedule some time to release old patterns and beliefs and to be more fully open to Light. Sit in prayer or meditation and connect with your breath. Drop your attention from your head into your heart. You can place your hands over your heart chakra to assist. If you are attuned to symbols, draw the Chokurei (Power Symbol) and Hen Sha Ze Shonen (Distance Symbol) in the air in front of you. If you are not yet attuned to symbols, hold the thought of connecting with Reiki energy and state the following intention with confidence and expectancy:

> May the Reiki Guides and Masters assist in the healing at the root cause of the sources of my anxieties, fears, and doubts in fully embracing Reiki in my daily life. I am open to being healed, expanded and aligned with the Reiki and Earth frequencies.

Sit in meditation for a minimum of 13 minutes (of the entire 20-30 allotted for this exercise), allowing the Reiki energies to move through you, cleansing your chakras. If you are experiencing brain chatter, do not wrestle with calming it – simply do not give it your attention and refocus on your breathing. When complete, give a prayer of thanks and then seal in your healing and the new energies by saying the following:

> I thank the Guides and Masters for their loving healing and expansion today. May this higher frequency of acceptance be sealed within and around me. I fully embrace and surrender to the Reiki Consciousness in my life.

Take a few moments to record your observations. With any meditation or Reiki experience, your intention is to simply 'notice what you notice' and not attempt to analyze or 'figure out' your experience. During and after the 13-day ritual, observe the changes in yourself and your Reiki awareness and abilities. Enjoy!

What are Crystals?

It is commonly believed that our Universe began with the 'Big Bang' explosion. Matter scattered across the Universe. Our Earth formed when denser and lighter bits of matter came together. As iron and nickel are heavier, they formed the Earth's core. The outer layer of the Earth is called the Crust, and it is less than one percent of the total mass of the Earth. The Crust is 40 kilometers thick at the most. In the upper part of the Crust, you find crystals, gemstones, and mined minerals.

A crystal is a solid body with a geometrically regular shape. The Oxford Dictionary states:

> *A crystal is a solid, symmetrical structure in which the atoms and molecules are packed in a regularly ordered, repeating pattern extending in all three spatial dimensions.*

In the formation of these structures, the crystal units stack perfectly without any gaps in between them. The shape and the atomic structure of a crystal define it. Crystals are lighter in color and much more transparent than minerals.

Another property, known as a 'defect' is important to the crystal healer. What is technically considered a defect, adds real potential to the healing properties of particular crystals. Some of my favorite 'defect' crystals for healing are those clear ones that contain minerals in a pattern known as occlusions. They are very powerful when working with any 'core of self' issues.

Minerals are defined as having a consistent, chemical structure and are very homogenous in nature. Often, they are mined for a specific purpose or use. Some of the characteristics of minerals are structure, hardness, shine, color and streaking, strength, how it breaks and its specific gravity. Minerals are denser in color and often heavier in weight than crystals. Think of gold or silver in comparison with a clear quartz crystal – the formers are minerals and quartz is a crystal. In this book, the term 'crystal' includes denser stones with defined healing properties.

The healing properties of minerals are vast, yet often undervalued by people using Earth tools for energy conduits. Their energy strengthens and heals the foundational elements of the body – the bones, blood, soft tissues, etc. You need a strong physical foundation and to be very grounded to the Earth for spiritual expansion that will not exhaust or deplete you. The energy of minerals supports and builds your inner core of strength and assist with grounding.

How Crystals are Formed

Most of Earth's crystals formed millions of years ago. The process they underwent while developing is important to their healing properties. Granite was formed when magma cooled very slowly (over millions of years), crystals found within granite are often not well formed.

Crystals are minerals that have had the chance to grow and shape just the way they were meant to be. As your DNA determines the color of your eyes, your height and bone structure, the chemicals that comprise a crystal or mineral, plus the pressure they are under and the geopathic forces present, determine its shape and energy-work capabilities. What is so amazing is that crystals of the same type have the same structure wherever found in the world!

Crystals created in a liquid environment are usually more well-formed. Liquid, such as magma and water, as well as gasses, are pushed up from deep in the Earth into cracks and crevices in the host rock structure. As the liquid evaporated, the high concentration of minerals within the water bonded together. Crystals formed as their component atoms moved closer and closer together. The development of a particular crystal is based on its chemical compound, the rate of evaporation of the liquid, the amount of heat and pressure from the rock around it and any erosion that occurs. The higher the temperature to which the elements are exposed, the harder the crystal becomes. Diamonds, rubies, sapphires and Herkimer diamonds form in some of the highest temperatures. Softer crystals such as halite (salt) and gypsum usually form in softer sedimentary rock. In 1812, the German mineralogist Friedrich Mohs created the Mohs' scale of hardness. This scale quantifies the scratch resistance of minerals by comparing the ability of a harder material to scratch a softer material ranging from talc (1) to diamond (10). You'll find the scale later in this book.

Other Influences Including Geopathic Stressors

There is brilliant, higher consciousness guiding the process of the formation of crystals. Whether hard or soft, and no matter what form they take, their crystalline structure can absorb, conserve, channel, activate, focus, and emit energy. This ability is what we tap into and align with as energy workers.

In working with crystals, people add the 'non-tangible influences.' These include the Reiki Frequency and your personal influences, beliefs, soul history and soul purpose as a healer, as well as your intentions with this work. Some tangibles influences added by humans include tumbling or shaping a crystal or enhancing the color and heat treating.

There is one more special feature that impacts the healing properties of a particular crystal. It is the geopathic stressors present during its formation. Geo means Earth and pathic means stress. The Earth has a natural electromagnetic field that is at a frequency of roughly 7.8 Hz. Our brain waves are optimal when in alignment with this frequency. Geopathic stress lines run through the Earth at a consistent interval. One of the most common theories is the Hartmann lines form a grid that generally follows the lines of longitude and latitude, and are approximately six feet apart.

The presence of an underground, geopathic stress line when a crystal or mineral forms impacts the energy and healing properties of that stone. Where multiple stress lines intersect, a real party happens! When it comes to the formation of crystals, the presence of geopathic stress can enable new and greater properties for a particular crystal to be present. Though the energy of a crystal or mineral is not scientifically measurable at this time, your intuition, Energy-testing skills (see upcoming directions) and your practical observations with a crystal over time will reveal its abilities. When I teach Reiki and Crystals, I do a blind energy test with students using at least ten different amethyst from different parts of the world. They do not see the crystals but describe their resonance and impressions when holding them. Their impressions and visions form patterns with the geographic home of a particular amethyst, and they are all amazed to find that they are all amethyst!

"Once formed, crystals are the most stable and
organized form of matter in the Universe."

~ Healing with Crystals and Chakra Energies

The New Frequency of Reiki and Crystals

We know that Reiki is the God-Consciousness made real on the Earth. We also know that crystals are ancient conduits of the Earth Consciousness. To determine their sum, you do not simply add these two facts together.

The twin-flame marriage of Reiki and Crystals in an intentional manner enables you to channel and use a much higher frequency of consciousness and healing. Know that Reiki in its present form has only been with us for less than a century. Human understanding of Reiki and its potential is really in its infancy. As the number of Reiki practitioners and Masters expands, this greater mass consciousness of Reiki will allow us to grasp and access more of its wisdom. In other words:

> *Our knowledge and ability of Reiki are not meant to be static. It is not meant to remain as Dr. Usui graciously presented it to our planet. The river of Reiki energy will continue to expand and evolve, with greater intensity and knowledge.*

The marriage of Reiki and Crystals enables a new frequency of energy to be activated for you to access, channel, heal yourself and others and to evolve the consciousness of Earth. Through this comes a greater release of Reiki Wisdom. Two of the greatest gifts of Reiki are that:

a. Reiki has its own wise consciousness, and

b. Reiki can never have a negative impact.

The wisdom inherent in Reiki knows what is required by the recipient and where its energy needs to go within their physical body, the auric field, and life. This wisdom provides incredible freedom for the Reiki practitioner, as she is not required to diagnose or analyze the experience for the client. She is open to using her intuition and intention to listen, assess, and gently direct the energies which further empowers their abilities to transform.

When Reiki is directed through crystals, Reiki's wisdom expands, and that of the practitioner grows with it. Both the Reiki energies and the practitioner align with the innate ability of the particular crystal, and boosts like magic the power of a particular stone. Amethyst's gentle, powerfully nurturing way intensifies. Bloodstone goes to the root of a person's anger and heals it. Rose quartz channels the deep love that the recipient requires.

The Earth holds a higher dimension of God-Consciousness, but since she is below our feet, she is not often perceived this way. The more grounded and Earth connected you are, the farther you can expand your consciousness in higher dimensions and realms.

The best Reiki practitioners and teachers have their feet
on the ground and their head in the heavens.

Activating crystalline energy with Reiki opens the door wide to accessing, using and being nurtured by the Earth force. Your learning here empowers you to:

⊚ Develop a strong relationship with the Earth Consciousness. Doing this ables you to hear her messages, channel her energies, become recharged and, in turn, be more grounded and centered as you move through your life.

◎ Channel the innately profound frequencies of light and healing found in the Earth and make it real for human use, healing and expansion.

◎ Connect with and use the energy of any crystal, mineral, stone or gem.

◎ Increase your ability to work with any other Earth-based energies, such as elementals, vortexes, geopathic lines, topographic features and bodies of water. (I am now able to bring in the energies of sacred sites around the world – even those I haven't visited in this lifetime)!

Tips for Working with Crystals and Reiki

This list provides you with the essentials to remember when working with the Reiki and Crystals Frequency. Use it as your 'go to' list or for a quick refresher when you need one.

1. Know that the moment you put a certain crystal, gem, mineral or element together with Reiki, the magic begins.

2. Intention is holding a 'focused purpose.' Once you are attuned to Reiki, your ability to focus your intention increases and is strengthened through embracing the Reiki consciousness. Intention is not about control. It is a moment in time where desire, possibility and thought come together in a state of Grace.

3. Learning the properties of crystals can become a lifetime passion. Avoid doubting yourself because you don't know it all. No one person knows it all! We are in a time where Earth energies are revealing more of their potential all the time, and this will continue indefinitely. Working with crystals from a place of intention and love with Reiki is the key.

4. If magic begins simply by putting together Crystals with Reiki, then adding the symbols moves you into a higher level of wizardry. The symbols are microcosms of the God Consciousness that humans can access, use and direct with intention. Wow!

5. Remember to cleanse your stones on a regular basis. With Reiki, the cleansing of crystals to release held energies is simplified, though knowing how to clear crystals from a particular 'family' is essential. (See additional information in this book).

6. When you cleanse crystals without using Reiki, the task is more complex. There are more limitations regarding what will cleanse a particular stone and how to do it. Reiki clears all crystals, as well as whatever other natural element you are using in energy work. Give your crystals and other healing tools Reiki on a regular basis. Infuse them with the symbols in your toolbox. Schedule a minimum of 15 minutes weekly for this, and you will unleash their limitless potential.

7. Honor your energy and needs while moving into this new realm of healing. Adjusting to this Frequency is a process. Each time you work with crystals and each time you read these words, you will expand with the Light you hold and your knowledge. If you find that you are becoming too energized while working with Reiki and Crystals, take a break. It is important to stay grounded and focused, and this Frequency of energy can at times be so powerful, that your physical body needs time to adapt to it.

8. Keep certain crystals in your collection solely for your use. Though you are in service to others, honoring your energetic needs is a priority. You need a home base of nurturing and divine connections to recharge your battery, be affirmed in your work and receive insights. Your personal crystals provide this for you. No matter how strong the urge is to use them for someone else – do not. Honor that these stones have chosen you to enhance your Lightworker abilities and connect you home.

9. When you begin to work more intently with Reiki and Crystals, you expand and evolve to working with fifth-dimensional energies. Your connection with all nature and the consciousness of the Earth Mother grows. The shift can sometimes take you by surprise. Simply revel in it. Trust your intuition and you'll learn how the Earth through crystals speaks to you.

10. In non-Reiki based crystal healing, often only quartz crystals can be programmed for a higher vibration and specific purpose. When using Reiki with Crystals, all crystals, minerals and stones can be programmed with amazing results. The properties and cut of a crystal influence the extent to which one can be used for a particular purpose – so having basic crystal knowledge, doing your research and trusting your intuition are the keys to success.

Left and Right Brain Learning

Through my extensive teaching of Reiki, of healing with crystals, I've observed that the people who embrace and instinctively know the power of this work approach it with both their right and left brain. The right brain is known as our 'creative side' yet for spiritual beings having a human experience it is so much more. We access the field of all consciousness and limitlessness through our right brain, including the fields of crystal and Earth energies. The process of the right brain accesses and receives information without trying or needing to block or analyze it.

Simply stated, the left brain functioning is our logical, rational organizer of life. It is designed to 'make sense of things' and to ensure that the foundation of our physical lives remains intact and thrives. The left brain can also try to block new learning that does not have tangible proof. Being able to recognize when this is happening is essential for a Lightworker. The following story illustrates this:

During a recent summer, my spouse and I were driving to visit friends at their cottage. As we drove through a town, what I call my 'spidey-senses' heightened before I saw the sign for a local rock shop. There was such a pull to visit it, but my logical mind convinced me otherwise. Shopping elsewhere, I separated from my husband. The pull again was to go to the rock shop, but again my mind convinced me that I would find him in the hardware store. Eventually calling him on his cell phone, I found him at the rock shop looking for me!

Entering the store, I felt a grace-filled pureness in the energy. Looking in the cases, it was clear that the quality of the stones there was exceptional. Asking the young clerk for two specific pieces, I saw the recognition of a fellow traveler in his eyes. One of the highlights of this visit was connecting with Selenite wands that contained Enhydros – water bubbles captured since the birth of this crystal.

Jason, the clerk, and I chatted in the way that people who are meant to connect converse. Within seconds, we were to the heart of the matter. He was surrounded his whole life by stones and crystals as his father is a geologist. Jason found himself rapidly opening to the metaphysics of crystals. He said, "I'm not surprised you walked in this morning. I was frustratingly thinking last night that I don't know where to go next with all of this." He continued by saying how he questions when he reads about what a crystal is 'supposed to do.' Where does this healing information come from?"

I responded: "I know what you are saying. We have both a left and a right brain too. As the right opens and expands to new awareness, the logical left needs to be satisfied. When you begin to look at crystals and feel and experience them in a new way, it challenges how you see everything. You soon realize that what you had learned to be reality or truth may not — and most often is not — what you believed."

A sense of relief washed over his face, and we continued to speak of the field of all possibility. Of course, I purchased several pieces that day which are exceptional in my work, and our chat has stayed with me and influenced my teaching.

Part II

The Tools in Your
Reiki and Crystals Toolbox

The G.R.A.G. Model

Activating Reiki and Crystals together enables a force that channels divine consciousness in a much stronger manner than either Reiki or Crystals on their own. This frequency allows for divine consciousness to work through this path, enabling expanded healing and access to all possibilities in the field of universal consciousness. Intention is the fuel that activates the new energies created with Reiki and Crystals together.

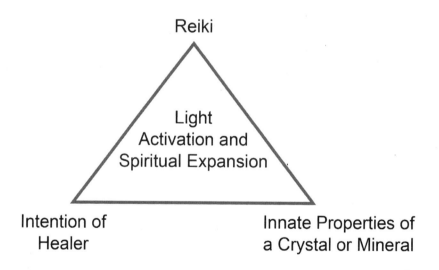

One day, while playing with some high vibrational crystals and placing Reiki symbols in them, I heard a voice say, "Teach them the model." After looking around to see if anyone was there, I realized I had experienced a moment of Grace in action where Guidance gave me a key. Of course, my very human response was "Model? What Model?" Then I saw in my mind's eye, the letters G.R.A.G.

The following weekend, I was teaching one of my first Reiki and Crystals classes. Suddenly, I knew I needed to pull out a flip chart and markers, and over the next 30 minutes, the G.R.A.G. Model appeared. Working backward from these four letters as I had first received them, it was revealed that the letters referred to the Generating, Receiving, Amplifying and Grounding properties of Reiki and Crystals together. These four properties are activated and fueled by the frequency that I was being given to channel.

The G.R.A.G. Model provides us with a framework to comprehend how to use this gift we are given. More in-depth information on each of these four properties follows in the next section. The intentions of this unique G.R.A.G Model given to us are:

⊙ Maximizing healing and learning

⊙ Accelerating healing and learning

⊙ Solidifying and integrating healing and learning

These categories aid learning and understanding in a systematic way when working with the Reiki and Crystal Frequency. Be aware of the flexibility of the categories and the potential for any particular crystal to fall into several categories.

#1 Generating

Think of a battery-powered generator that you use when the electricity goes out. It is a self-contained unit that is much more powerful than its compact size. Within is stored the potential for great relief and lighting the way in the darkest of times.

The generating property of the Reiki and Crystals Frequency does much the same. Through this property, you can take a very small and even unappealing stone and enable a powerhouse for energy generation and healing. When using Reiki and Crystals as Generators, you:

- Maximize the crystal or stone's innate ability to generate energy and store it for a specific purpose

- Provide a conduit for Reiki energy to build and flow with intention

- Store Reiki energies within the crystal or stone, activating them to build and grow

- Direct channeled energies to flow with intention

You are the catalyst for a powerful healing force to be unleashed and focused.

Creating a Reiki Generator

There are crystals known for their inherent ability to generate energy. Any Earth element can become a Reiki-Crystal generator, but choosing one that has the built-in ability is a great place to start.

The shape of the crystal you are using is key. It is best to choose a single-terminated crystal, where one end is more rounded or flat and on the other end all facets converge to a point. Wands with a pointed end are also optimal for this purpose. Here is the process for building generating energy within your crystal:

1. Be sure that it has been cleansed since last use (see instructions in this book).

2. Activate the generating properties before a session or while your client is present.

3. Hold in both hands, and ask the Reiki Guides to assist in activating your crystal to generate Reiki energy.

4. Add any symbols that you may know. Also, allow any other symbols that come into your awareness to enter the crystal. The Chokurei, or Power Symbol, is a very powerful Reiki symbol in building the energies in a generating crystal. Its inherent meaning is: Put All the Power of the Universe Here.

5. To use, focus on the area of the body chakra or energy field that holds your attention. Know that this may not be near the problem area or energy blockage that the client identifies.

6. Visualize or think about all the energies built within the crystal rushing out the crystal's tip and into the area for the client's highest good.

7. You can ask for Guidance on how to energetically proceed. Generator energy has its own consciousness and great power, and will lead you where you need to go – as long as you don't try to mentally 'figure out' what it is conveying. It will speak to you through your intuitive, heart-based knowing.

> *Crystals used for generating energy demonstrate the inherent meaning for the Power Symbol (Chokurei): Put all of the power of the Universe here.*

#2 Receiving

All crystals receive, yet some have been divinely structured to do so more readily. Their source location, chemical structure, and shape all contribute to this ability. Like a person who channels, he or she has antennae that are built, programmed and tuned in to receive energy that can be used for self or communicated to others. A receiver crystal does the same.

Built to receive, it translates what you require from higher vibrational sources for your highest good in the third-dimensional world. This process of translation is very complex. What is sent to us from higher dimensions arrives in a pattern of light. While in human form, our ability to interpret light signals is very limited. Receiving crystals provide the assistance required to receive this light information, interpret and translate it, and then put it in a form for our human use. Here is a list of possible uses, yet using crystals as receivers for healing is as limitless as you are:

- Access higher realms of information and healing frequencies

- Connects you with your Guides and those of your clients

- Enables you to access the Fifth-Dimensional realm of the Ascended Masters and their knowledge

- Conduit for new and channeled information

- Receiving new information for client in regards to their healing and development needs

- Receiving new information for you as a healer, for personal growth and on your spiritual journey

⊚ Holding Reiki energy to be released later and through distance healing

A receiver crystal is often from the quartz family but do not let this limit your choices. Know that mechanically shaped crystals are also great to use. I have a set of five clear quartz in sacred geometry patterns that I use when anchoring a client with the Fifth Dimensional Frequency. Other shapes such as balls, pyramids, ovals, and animals are often great for receiver crystals. To help with choosing a particular crystal for receiving, research its inherent properties and assess how that fits with your intended purpose. The Energy-testing directions found in this book are also helpful. In the final section of this book, you will find a list of Advanced Crystals for Channeling. These are all considered receiver stones.

> *Crystals used for receiving energy and information demonstrate the inherent meaning of the Mental-Emotional Symbol (Say Hee Kee) meaning Great Beam of Light Shine on me and be my Friend.*

Programming a Crystal with Reiki

Programming comes from pure intention. You have a powerful tool to focus your energy and the assistance you are receiving through the crystal and from spiritual helpers so that all work optimally together for your intended purpose.

Simply open your Reiki toolbox and your crystal resources and start to play! Think as 'big as you can' about what you desire to achieve and trust that it will occur. Choose from your Reiki tools (e.g. symbols, healing attunements) and enhance the crystal with them before healing or channeling. Be very clear with your intention – state it aloud even if you are the only one present!

You will be heard by your Guides, and the results will be optimal and magnificent.

#3 Amplifying

When you listen to a band, amplifiers make the music louder. Think of this with the amplifying properties of crystals when infused with Reiki. Their inherent properties have a stronger vibration and tone, expanding their known abilities and revealing hidden ones. In their brilliant way, amplifying with crystals digs deep. With clients, they bring to the surface in a person the source of an energy blockage, move out pain, and reveal the truth. My intention in healing work is always to go after the root cause, no matter how deeply hidden. Amplifying crystals readily reveal the root cause, allowing my work to be much easier and thorough. Choose colored stones that are more vibrant and less dense in mass. Know this about crystals for amplifying energy:

- They are naturals with working in the realms of magick. They reveal what is hidden and identify issues, translating them for human understanding.

- In the process of healing and expansion, a person outgrows energy patterns and beliefs that once served them. Amplifying stones with Reiki are catalysts for releasing what is no longer helpful.

- Blockages and old energies arise to the surface.

- Crystals that have the inherent ability to shield and protect your energy are made significantly stronger.

- Clear energy, even when quite toxic, from a person or room.

Amplifying crystals are often the ones that attract your attention in your heart center. Feel them out with your heart, and you'll see their unique potential. Some of my favorites are kunzite, selenite, golden healer, moldavite, pink tourmaline, and celestite. With Reiki, their amplified properties are so powerful that I rarely place them on a person above the space between the heart and throat chakras.

> *Crystals used for amplifying demonstrate the meaning of the Distance Symbol (Hon Sha Ze Shonen): May the Buddha in me meet the Buddha in you to promote Peace and Harmony*

Amplifying with a Double-Terminated Crystal

These types of crystals come with a naturally formed point at both ends, with a straighter body between the two points. With Reiki, you can put the symbols in the crystal, and then hold the point towards the recipient while drawing the symbols. Doing this amplifies the crystal's ability and focuses them in a laser-like way, making them exceptionally powerful for psychic surgery.

Using double-terminated crystals is as limitless as you are. Here are some of their potential uses that you can boost with the intentional use of Reiki and by adding symbols:

- Radiating internal energy out both ends

- Drawing energy in from both ends

- Dissolving negative energy

There are two great methods available to us to increase the flow of energies from both ends of a double-terminated crystal:

a. Hold the crystal in your hand and think of Reiki while you do so. If you are attuned to Reiki symbols, draw them over the crystal and tap them in. When placing the crystal on or near a person, draw Reiki symbols or simple circles over the area of focus, thinking of the process as being supercharged.

b. For psychic surgery, hold one point of the crystal towards the recipient. Over the other end draw the Reiki symbols and guide them with your eyes and your intention through the crystal. Pretend that you are an etheric surgeon, working deep with the body and removing energetic blockages. Though never touching the person, you are removing the energy that is holding the issue in place.

Be aware of the crystal's placement and your intention of where you draw from and where the energy then goes. When using a double-terminated crystal to extract an energy blockage from an area of the body, never point the other end of the crystal towards your palm chakra. You don't want to pick up what is released! Think with intention as to where you would like this energy to go. In my office, I've constructed an etheric volcano to receive and recycle heavy or negative energy, so I think of the energy leaving the double-terminated crystal and going directly to the volcano for recycling.

#4 Grounding

After 20 years of teaching advanced energy work and on my miracle-filled journey, grounding stones have been a best friend. Crystals and stones that ground you:

◎ Hold you and your clients to the Earth so that the highest Source energy can be received.

◎ Never waver in feeding your root chakra, which must be strong to do healing work.

◎ Strengthen the foundation of your whole life, enabling strong relationships and the ability to expand energetically.

◎ Heal you, providing the foundation for being 'Spirit in the Flesh.'

◎ Enable you to connect more readily with the Fifth Dimension and the Oneness of All.

◎ Bring inner peace where darker emotions and toxicity are present.

◎ Enable you to move forward and expand energetically.

When teaching beginner students, I often hear little comments (a.k.a. complaints) that I spend too much time focusing on grounding when they want to fly! I just keep repeating "You must have your feet on the ground and your head in the heavens." Time and again, I hear such gratitude from Masters and Fifth-Dimensional students for my insistence on their learning great grounding techniques early! The reason is:

> *You can only expand spiritually and consistently hold a powerful vibration as much as you can stay in your core of self and remain connected to the Earth.*

One of our great challenges is that we are rapidly being given the ability to access Source energy and frequencies of Light, yet have a great learning curve as how to manage this energy physically and use the gifts given in daily life. Being able to do this is essential for remaining spiritually strong, and not experiencing the yo-yo of highs and lows so common for Lightworkers. Only in grounded expansion can you heal karma and live your soul purpose.

These denser, darker-colored grounding stones must be included in any work or play you do with Reiki and Crystals. The Frequency you'll be channeling has great strength, so you need to anchor to the Earth. Put denser and colored stones on the floor of your treatment space by your feet when you're self-healing and keep them on you through the day. Place a grounding stone between the feet of a client you are assisting. Any time you use, wear, or activate a crystal programmed to the highest frequencies, have a partner stone connecting you to the Earth, keeping your root chakra strong and balanced.

> *Think of Mother Earth using her best mom voice, telling you to listen up and not break this rule! You'll be grateful for this as you uncover and discover the power available through the Reiki and Crystals Frequency.*

Suggested grounding stones are black mica, jasper, carnelian, black tourmaline, calcite, smoky quartz, and dark amethyst. Avoid malachite, hematite and obsidian for grounding. When using the Reiki and Crystals Frequency, they can be more energetically volatile and inconsistent with grounding.

> *Crystals used for grounding demonstrate the meaning of the Master Symbol (Dai Ko Myo): May God and Humanity become One.*

Common Crystal Terminology

When you move into the world of crystals, stones and minerals, it is easy to feel overwhelmed. Part of this is that there is a new language to learn. The following will provide you with a great foundation before we move forward. Knowing these terms will also assist you in making optimal choices and buying decisions!

Agate: Quartz from the chalcedony family whose colors form in bands or groups. If found in a geode the pattern is exposed when sliced in half. If very brightly colored, this has been done by heat treating and/or a dyeing process that can affect the energy of the stone.

Cathedral Crystal: A crystal cluster where there is one dominant point and other points rising up, almost parallel to the major one. Smaller crystals can rise up next to the secondary points.

Chunks: Crystals without notable facets. Good for enriching a room's atmosphere, for holding during meditation or simply carrying with you for ongoing benefit. The non-clear ones are often great for grounding.

Cleavage: The weakness in a crystal so that it naturally breaks along a certain angle or line to keep its shape.

Clusters: A group of small crystals that have naturally grown joined. They are excellent for enriching a living environment or workplace. Depending upon the properties of a particular cluster, it can cleanse, invigorate or calm an environment.

Crystal Clusters: Are formations of single terminated crystals. Place a crystal cluster to create a stronger healing vibration or to purify an area of negative vibrations. Used to purify and recharge other crystals, healing stones or jewelry by simply placing them on the cluster for at least three hours.

Cut Crystals: Cut crystals have been cut and polished into shapes such as pyramids, wands or spheres, which can make them very attractive. If they are well-cut, the energy of the stone can be maintained and often amplified. Vogel crystals are cut to the specifications outlined by the late Marcel Vogel. Each type of Vogel crystal has different healing purposes.

Double-Terminated Crystals: With these, you will find a single point at both ends where the six facets join. For healing and channeling energy, these crystals are very versatile though require the user to be very mindful. As energy can enter and exit both ends of the crystals, you need to keep in mind how the energy naturally flows based on the shape in regards to the results you desire. It is not about trying to control a double-terminated crystal's inherent abilities, but rather to reign it in and guide it for its highest good. (See the G.R.A.G. Model section on amplifying with a double-terminated crystal).

Enhydro: A bubble of water trapped inside a crystal since its formation. They are becoming rarer to obtain, so if one crosses your path, take it home! These crystals are very helpful for high vibrational healing and scrying work.

Elestials: These chunk-like stones have many terminations and folds over a multi-layered crystal. Elestials have a very high vibration. If one shows up, take notice!

Facet: The face or side of a crystal. It can be naturally occurring or shaped by a machine.

Gemstones: A crystal or mineral deemed to be valuable, and cut and polished for use in jewelry or display.

Generator Crystals: Single Quartz crystals that can vary in size used in healing to intensify the energy that the healer channels for self or a client. You can direct the energy by placing the point where you would like the energy to flow. Six facets come together to form an apex and sometimes there are cloudiness or inclusions. These are very powerful tools, especially when used with Reiki. (See the G.R.A.G. Model for more information).

Geode: Found in a ball or sphere, they are thick and crusty on the outside. When cut open, they are often filled with crystals and the walls are crystalline points. Geodes with clear quartz crystal walls are good for clearing other stones by placing them inside.

Inclusion: Appears as though it may be a flaw in the body of the crystal. In crystal healing work, inclusions enhance healing being done. Crystals with inclusions are powerful allies for healing. Trust their higher purpose. When used with Reiki, crystals with inclusions are highly programmable and often bring through high-level non-Reiki energies as well.

Irradiation: This process uses radioactive rays to modify or brighten the color of a crystal. Some gemstones have always been irradiated, such as blue topaz. But, many crystals are being irradiated to modify their appearance and color as well, so you may not be buying what you think you are or purchasing crystals with reduced energy. Always ask the original source location of a crystal, especially if it is exceptionally attractive.

Laser Quartz: Long and thin, energy concentrates and accelerates through it like a tight beam or laser. Often used as a psychic surgery tool.

Matrix: The host rock within which a crystal or mineral is found.

Occlusion: Deposits of another mineral within a crystal, that can appear as a smaller crystal inside the larger one.

Opaque: A crystal or mineral that no light can pass through.

Phantoms: Inclusions within crystals – usually appear as a shadow, shape, face or cloudy striation. If one has come across your path, it has not done so by chance.

Piggy-back or Dolphin: A smaller quartz crystal attached to a larger one as if it is sitting on its back. These are very powerful healing tools.

Rainbow: When light refracts through a clearer quartz crystal you see rainbow colors in one or more places within the stone. These are powerful crystals, especially for gaining higher knowledge. Look for clear quartz crystals with rainbows for healing, as they are a natural gateway for accessing realms of magick and other dimensions for healing.

Record Keepers: On one side of the crystal, there is a symbol – often a triangle – that formed naturally on the crystal's surface. The symbol is small and finding one is rare. These crystals carry high vibration energy and messages.

Single-Terminated Crystals: With these crystals, you will find a single point at one end, and a rough or rounded edge at the other. Be mindful of the point's direction when using it in healing work as the energy flows in and out of the point. For example, if your intention is to move excess energy from the head to the feet (to ground them), then you would always have the point directed to their feet.

Tabular Crystals: Flat crystals (two of the opposing six sides are much wider) often formed by a machine. Very good healing tools as they lay flat on the body. Tabulars are often used to balance the energies between any two elements, such as two chakras. They often have a deeply nurturing, calming effect on the area where applied.

Termination: It is the point at the end of a crystal and can be round, pointed or flat. Double-terminated crystals have faces that join together to form a point on both ends.

Translucent: Some light can pass through it.

Transparent: Light can pass through the crystal or stone.

Tumbled Stones: Easily found for sale, they are smaller rocks or crystals that have been tumbled over each other many times with increasingly finer abrasive until the sides become smooth and shiny.

Vug: It is a hollow space in a rock where crystals have formed. It is also one of my favorite, uncommon words to use when playing Scrabble!

Wand: It is a long, round-shaped tool for healing made of crystal or mineral that assists the healer to direct energy. A wand can be single- or double-terminated, and may or may not be smooth on the outside. Usually, your wand chooses you!

Cleansing and Recharging Crystals with Reiki

As a Reiki practitioner, you do have a 'natural shield' to negativity. Yet, before using or wearing any crystal, cleanse it. Crystals are active absorbers of energy. If a crystal has been handled or displayed before you have it, it will still contain the residual energies of others. If you wear or use it prior to cleansing, this residual energy can leach into your energy field or that of the person you are assisting. Here is a great tip: when holding a stone that has not been cleansed, do so in your right hand if you are right-handed, as we receive with the left. For left-handed people, this is not reversed one hundred percent, so use your intuitive knowing to decide.

There are certain crystals that never need cleansing such as kyanite, selenite and super seven. Researching how a particular stone should be cleansed is always helpful. When a new crystal or holder of Earth energies has come to you, immediately put Reiki and symbols into it to neutralize stored energies and align it with you.

How-to Cleanse Crystals

With Reiki: Use symbols to which you've been attuned and put them into a crystal with the intention of cleansing them thoroughly. Breathe in and draw Power Symbol (Chokurei) on the roof of your mouth. Direct your out-breath to the crystal, thinking of how the breath and the symbol are clearing it. When cleansing, be sure to include the

Mental-Emotional symbol, or Say Hee Kee, as it is very powerful for cleansing emotional, energetic debris. Ask Spirit that the released, old energy be returned to Mother Earth for recycling.

Visualization: Through your Reiki learning, you've experienced that time and distance is not a fixed construct. You can send energy anywhere, and you are also able to pull energy in from anywhere.

You can cleanse and charge your crystals this way: hold the stone that you wish to clear in your hands then begin to meditate asking the Reiki Guides for assistance. Then connect with a sacred site, such as Mt. Kurama, Japan (where Dr. Usui met Reiki), the vortexes of Sedona, the otherworldly energy of Machu Picchu or Stonehenge. Choose any site that calls to you, permitting the sacred energies to infuse you and the stone. You'll be amazed at the journey you will have and how your crystal will vibrate!

Smudging: This powerful ritual that comes through Aboriginal traditions releases what is no longer required and heals and calls in divine assistance. Often used for smudging are sage, frankincense, sandalwood, cedar, sweet grass, and incense. When called to smudge a crystal, I also include other approaches on this list.

Running water: Hold your crystals in cold running water and visualize the current energetic state of the stone being washed away. How long you choose to immerse your crystal is largely intuitive, as there is no correct amount of time. A natural stream or river is preferable for this method, but tap water will do as well. The natural salinity of ocean water is also an excellent cleanser.

Research if water is a safe cleansing method for your crystal. Certain stones that are very soft, layered in structure or porous, such as selenite, deteriorate in water. Water cleansing can damage any crystal with less than a 4 rating on the Mohs Scale, such as opal or pearls.

Brown Rice: Allow the crystals to rest on brown rice for 24 hours. It balances and transmutes negative energy.

Table Salt: Check with a crystal source guide if salt is safe with your particular crystal. Avoid using salt – wet or dry – with any stones that are porous, have cracks on the surface, or are less than a 4 rating on the Mohs Scale. I rarely use table salt for cleansing.

Saltwater: Best to use sea salt. For the size of a cereal bowl, you would use one heaping teaspoon in water, so adjust according to the container you are using. Rest the stones in the saltwater bath for at least an hour and place in sunlight if you are able. Infuse the water with Reiki symbols and energy by holding your hands over it for five minutes at the start of the cleansing. Use the same guidelines as under the table salt heading.

Dry Salt: Resting your crystals in a sea salt bed for 24 hours powerfully transmutes negative energy. Always be sure to remove any residue from the surface of your stone, as salt can squeeze into tiny crevices or scratch the surface. Use the same guidelines as under the table salt heading.

Earth Cleansing: Burying a crystal in the Earth gives it an opportunity to regenerate completely. Much like other cleansing methods, use your intuition to guide how long to leave it. A longer period is often optimal here, so consider one to two weeks. Increase the impact by burying and unearthing your crystals during the full moon, new moon, equinoxes, or other galactic events.

Burying is particularly good for grounding Earth element stones like smoky quartz and tourmaline, which have a tendency to absorb negativity from their environment. Wrapping softer stones in plastic before burying will not impact the cleansing process and will protect your stones. If you do not have access to outdoor space, use a plant pot with clean soil in it. If using this method, be sure that the stones are not porous or soft. Reiki the site and add symbols often.

Sound Vibrations: Tibetan bells, drumming, tuning forks, and singing bowls are also helpful cleansing aids. As their energy output is slightly different than other methods (being waveform in nature), they are less inhibited by physical barriers, and can penetrate the crystalline structure. Speak the names of the Reiki symbols while using sound vibration for healing, with the intention that they travel on the sound waves into the stone.

Intention: Pure intention is an extremely powerful force. While holding your crystal in your hands, visualize white light surrounding your crystal, beaming from the inside out. In your mind or aloud, affirm positively that your stone is a clear and perfect channel of energy. Infuse the crystal with Reiki symbols.

Sunlight: Placing your crystals near a window allows the sun to work its therapeutic magic. The varying wavelengths of light throughout the day give full spectrum vibrational healing to stones.

A few cautions here: clear quartz balls or prisms can focus the sun's rays and become a fire hazard. Some crystals will fade in sunlight. These include amethyst, citrine, fluorite, and artificially colored stones such as agate slices.

Moonlight: This is most powerful during the full moon and new moon. Place your crystals outside, and overnight if possible.

Using a Recharger

Though all forms of cleansing recharge your crystals, intentionally charging them takes this a step further. To charge the crystal with

Reiki, hold the stone in your hands and feel the Reiki energy flow into it. If you have symbols, draw the Chokurei, Say Hee Kee and Hon Sha Ze Shonen into it as well.

One of my personal shortcuts to cleansing is having a larger stone with a higher vibration, such as selenite, kunzite or a larger clear quartz cluster and designate it as a 'recharger stone.' While activating the recharger stone with Reiki, the rule is that when you place other crystals on or near it that they will be cleansed and charged to their highest vibration. Then I leave the stones on or near it for at minimum several hours. Fill your recharger stone with Reiki and symbols weekly. Thank it for its service! Here is the bar of Selenite I use in my Reiki room:

The Mohs Scale of Hardness

The Mohs scale provides us with a comparative chart to understanding the hardness of a mineral. It was invented by Austrian mineralogist Friedrich Mohs in 1812 by taking ten minerals of differing hardness (below), and evaluating how easily the surface can be altered or scratched relative to each other. The differences are not meant to be consistent between numbers, as the hardness between nine and ten is greater than the hardness of all of one through eight.

1	*Talc*	Can be scratched with a fingernail
2	*Gypsum*	Can be scratched with a fingernail
3	*Calcite*	Can be scratched with a copper coin
4	*Fluorite*	Easily scratched with a knife
5	*Apatite*	Can be scratched with a knife
6	*Orthoclase*	Can be scratched with a steel file
7	*Quartz*	Can scratch window glass
8	*Topaz*	Can scratch Quartz
9	*Corundum*	Can scratch Topaz
10	*Diamond*	Can scratch Corundum and proves it's a diamond

Energy-Testing Technique

Applied Kinesiology is the technique where a healing professional asks a person's body a question and receives an answer through the resistance the body provides, usually with an arm or a leg. Seeing this for the first time can challenge the logical mind. The body's biological intelligence is being asked a question to indicate the source of an issue or what is for a person's highest good. The human body holds all of the answers for what it requires for wellness and wholeness. This technique uncovers the answers.

As you know, energy flows through the body. When there is resistance or blocked energy, the nervous system responds with weakness. In Energy-testing, this is indicative of a 'no' response. Through asking your body a question and assessing the level of strength the body provides, your body provides a 'yes' response. Know that the more specific and clear your question, the more that will be revealed. Examples of the types of questions you can ask include: the percentage of energetic function of an organ or system in the body, the frequency and amount of a particular supplement or remedy that is required, or even food sensitivities and the amount of a type of food that your body can manage. This approach is a gold-mine when working with crystals. Next, you'll learn Energy-testing to assist with your work with crystals. These skills will transform your entire life!

Using a crystal or metal pendulum can be used for Energy-testing. This approach is a form of dowsing, where one asks for yes or no answers to specific questions. For me, pendulum work has not resonated, though many people find it essential in their work. I've always used the Energy-testing approach described here as I always have my two hands and intuitive knowing with me. You can find many references online as to how to use a pendulum, and much of what I will share with you about Energy-testing will assist you with mastering pendulum work as well.

Energy-Testing Answers in Daily Life

Every day for over 20 years, I've used energy-testing. This constant for me in my life has been an unwavering friend providing clarity with the optimal nature of decisions, the source of an issue or illness or asking what my body requires. Being a Sensate, I can easily be overwhelmed by the energy in a crystal shop, and Energy-testing cuts through the myriad of options found there. Using Energy-testing, I can choose the optimal stone for myself and others – which saves an incredible amount of time, money and validates my inner knowing. In my work with crystals, being able to assess quickly which crystals or stones need cleansing, which one to use for a person or myself and exactly where to place it on or near the body improves the quality and speed of what I do. In my home, I use Energy-testing to assess the energetic flow and where to place crystals to cleanse or enhance the environment.

Energy-testing has been invaluable to my family, friends, and clients. First, learn and use this technique for yourself, and as you become more proficient and confident, use it when assisting others. In the approach you are learning here, you use your hands to test and provides you with information. Using this approach not only provides you with information and direction, but it also expands your internal guidance system. With practice, your self-awareness and inner-knowing will become stronger and more refined which allows the Guides to work through you more clearly. Over time, you will learn how to know what is for your highest good, and often be able to do so internally – without having to lift a finger!

How to Energy-Test

You have everything you need with your own two hands. (If you are physically unable to use your hands, you can use much of this information to develop your way of asking for information). The key fingers to use are the thumb and ring finger (the one next to the pinky) of both hands.

The following are the directions for energy-testing. Instructions and pictures shown are for a right-handed person. Please reverse if you left-hand dominant:

a. Touch together your ring finger and thumb on your left hand, flattening the two top pads together. Next, touch together the ring finger and thumb on your right hand, again flattening the two top pads together. You will notice how you create a circle between your fingers.

b. Put the fingers touching on the left hand inside the circle of the fingers touching on right hand.

c. While holding the outer right-hand circle together, gently separate the left-hand fingers inside the circle. Use gentle pressure to stop the outside circle right-hand fingers from

separating. This is how your 'yes' answer looks and feels when you ask a question.

d. Repeat, putting the left-hand fingers inside the right-hand finger circle. This time, allow the outer circle fingers on your right hand to release and separate under the force of the pressure caused by separating the inner fingers. This is how a 'no' answer looks and feels when you ask a question.

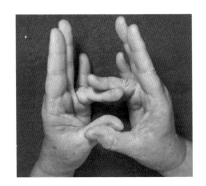

Energy-Testing Practice Exercises

Before energy-testing:

✓   Check in with yourself. Is your logical mind trying to figure out how this works or telling you that you cannot do this? Do not listen and focus on your breath.

✓   Bring your awareness to your whole self, with the focus coming from your heart chakra center.

✓   Are your feet flat on the floor and connected to the Earth? If not, plant yourself as this will assist with the clarity of your responses.

✓   Drink some water before beginning as being dehydrated will affect the accuracy of the responses you receive.

Essential to success with Energy-testing is the quality of the questions that you ask. Know that you are only asking questions that will have a 'yes' or 'no' response. Keep your questions in the present moment. Once you are proficient, you can ask about the past or future, but know that future results are less accurate.

The following are some practice questions. Notice how all of the questions can only have a yes or no answer. When you begin to ask your own questions, you need to word them so you will only have a yes or no response. So you can begin to understand how this technique can transform your whole life and work, we'll begin with questions about food supplements and personal decisions before moving on to crystals and healing. Here are some examples of questions worded for optimal results:

With Food or Supplements

Hold or place a food item or supplement bottle with contents inside as close as you can to your solar plexus and ask:

1. "For me, is this optimal for me to eat/take?" Yes? No? If still not sure ask "For me, is this detrimental for me to eat/take?" Yes? No?

2. "Is this food best hot?" "Is this food best room temperature?" "Is this food best cold?" Ask Yes? No? with each until you have your answer.

3. As you become proficient, you can begin to ask specific amounts that your body requires or tolerates.

With Personal Decisions

1. Think about your options, make a list and write them down.

2. Use Energy-testing to ask yes or no for each option individually. Write down your yes or no answer next to each option.

3. With each yes, use a scale of 0 (least) to 10 (most optimal) asking for the number to indicate how optimal now. The higher the number you receive a yes response to, the most optimal the answer.

The Quadrant Technique with Personal Health

1. Think of your body as four separate quadrants of upper right and left and lower right and left. You may want to draw the outline of your body on a page and divide into four parts indicating the four quadrants.

2. Ask "Where is the source of the issue in my body?" focusing on one quadrant at a time and asking yes and no. (It may not be where the pain or issue appears.)

3. Continue by asking more specific yes or no questions to receive further information.

4. You can then begin to ask questions to discern what your body requires. It is helpful is to think in a way that includes a variety of options that only have yes or no answers. This step is great to repeat over time as your body heals or evolves.

Energy-Testing and Crystals

When you begin to see how powerful this energy-testing tool is, you will readily use it when working with crystals. Begin by identifying the issue, an area of the body or personal energy field where you would like to include crystal healing. As with previous examples, you can ask yes and no questions to determine which crystal or stone (or a combination of) is optimal to use and where on the body. All crystals and minerals have a field of energy that always keeps it connected to the Earth and expands from within to around it, like an aura. Until you are comfortable with the field of energy of a particular crystal – and this comes with repetitive practice and exposure to them – you will get the best results by having the crystal(s) before you. Here are some examples using this powerful technique in your work with Reiki and Crystals:

1. Have before you the crystals, stones or minerals that you wish to use. (Don't worry if you have only a few – the optimal one will be there).

2. Knowing the area of the body, energy field or the issue you would like to address is helpful. If you intuitively sense it, that's great. If not, then use the quadrant technique to discern where the optimal quadrant is on the body or energy field.

3. Put the potential crystals in a row. Begin Energy-testing. Use the index finger of the right hand (if right-handed) and point to each crystal individually while asking the question "Is this one optimal to use?"

4. Notice which have a yes answer. Separate them from the rest.

5. Ask for the yes group "Do I use them all?" If you receive a no answer, ask, "Which ones do I use?" Point to each individually as you ask that question.

Keys for Healers

For some energy workers, using the word 'healer' to describe oneself does not always resonate. This belief often stems from knowing that the healing energies come through the practitioner from Source, and he or she is simply a magnificent conduit for healing energies. Those chosen (and who choose) to do this work can be miraculous catalysts and channels for the change or expansion for people, animals, nature or world situations. If you sometimes experience discomfort calling yourself 'healer,' accept that there is not any better word to describe what you provide so that others will understand.

What a Healer Does

A healer eases suffering and brings in joy, light, and hope for a person who is often exhausted by challenges and not thinking clearly about who they are and what they are experiencing then. People come for healing for many reasons, yet the driving force for seeing you is usually one of three reasons:

1. The first is to stop whatever is causing discomfort at the time. People don't often come until they are in a rather desperate chronic state of pain, illness or confusion and seek a way out or way through it all.

2. The person you are working with is often experiencing great vulnerability in their life and are choosing you to assist them on

the road back to health, perspective, growth and their core of self. In Reiki teaching, this is not stressed enough. When a person trusts a practitioner enough to assist in their hour of need, this is a great honor. That means in your role as a healer you need to be hyper-vigilant with your integrity, professionalism, knowledge, and intention in doing the work.

3. The inner push by their Soul's need is the third reason a person seeks Reiki assistance. The Soul knows when it is time for new expansion. The person may often arrive with a physical or emotional complaint, yet there is always another higher purpose for their need to consult with you. Here is the best explanation that I have observed over twenty years for this process:

    Everyone incarnates with soul purposes. For those who are Lightworkers, a spiritual timeline is illuminated within. This spiritual timeline embraces all that a person has been and are meant to become in all lifetimes. The energy of their timeline in this life, partners with what the person has contracted to attain, learn and be in this lifetime (before conception). The more one is committed to the process of expansion, the more brightly his or her spiritual timeline activates.

    Spontaneous downloads of information and energy occur to match a soul's learning needs. The more one is committed, the more one will receive. The opening of this door can never be closed – no matter how hard a person's toxic ego tries.

Through receiving attunements and light activations, studying energy work and spirituality, connecting with other Lightworkers, and choosing to live free of toxic fear, you will move rapidly along your spiritual timeline.

This journey does have its bumps and bruises. Deep inner clearing and healing of whatever limits your expansion is uncomfortable at times. When challenged by this process, it is time for you to seek assistance from trained energy workers. The energy embedded in this book and the teachings within are moving you along your spiritual timeline.

The greater your commitment to your healing and role as being in service to others, the more people will come to you seeking assistance. When a person trusts you enough to enter intimately into their energy field and touch their soul, it is a great act of courage on their part. And in this, know that the Universe is recognizing who you are and how far you have come.

Tools for Strength as a Healer

Whether you are seeing someone for healing or spiritual expansion (or both), your role is not to be taken lightly. Know that you are a channel for divine intervention in their life. Being in the role of healer for a person requires you to know and remember some key elements:

1. **Be Objective Rather than Subjective:** You both have different roles in the dance of healing. Your role in coming together with them is to be the catalyst for energy through you. You are the giver and they the receiver. The focus is on them, and it is not the time or place to discuss your issues. Keep a higher vision in your work with them, knowing that there is a boundary between the two of you. You are separate from the client yet energetically connected.

2. **Be Nonjudgmental:** Being nonjudgmental means you receive that person with an open heart, and with an open mind. You

do not judge what brought them there, who they are, and what choices they have made and will make in moving forward. Avoid using the word 'why' when asking them questions. Hidden in this word are the energies of blame and shame. Always know that it is their life and their journey.

3. **Do not Give Advice:** Too often I've observed healers over-stepping boundaries and giving advice or telling a client what to do. Even if you have had the same life experience, you are not the expert in their life. Also, if you are not a registered or licensed psychotherapist or counselor, it is beyond your training to provide any form of counseling. And, more than likely, it is against the law in your area to be counseling as part of your work.

   You will gain awareness and insight when working in the energy field of another. Clearly state your awareness and knowledge to the person you are working with, doing it in a way where they can hear it with clarity and purpose. Make sure that whatever insights or information you communicate is given in a mindful, purposeful way. Most clients want you to provide answers, but that is not your job. For growth, they need to uncover and discover their own answers.

   > One of the most striking issues I've observed with those doing healing work is that they move from simply receiving information and insights to interpreting, judging or analyzing what that information means for the client. That information, and how a client moves forward with it, can only be assessed by the person receiving it.

4. **Go only as Far as You are Comfortable:** You have the right only to assist people with whom you feel comfortable. Feeling comfortable includes listening to your inner voice telling you when a

person's issues are beyond the scope of your abilities or experience. Ask yourself "Am I the optimal fit for a person?"

Accept your training limitations so you do not go where you have not been taught to go. A great example of this is in seeing someone for Reiki, who is experiencing active mental health issues, such as being in a manic phase or suicidal. With the former, Reiki, and especially work with high vibration crystals, can make their symptoms worse. With someone who is suicidal, they require professional (medical) attention with a specialist in the field until their crisis has passed. My suggestion is never to be the primary treatment provider for anyone who is experiencing mental health extremes or crises unless you are trained to do so, and are part of a larger mental health team.

5. **Boundaries and Confidentiality are Essential:** We are all inter-connected in the Oneness of All. Always remember that the person for whom you are assisting is separate from yourself. When doing Reiki, you can often experience a sense of formlessness or a sense of soul connection with the person you are assisting. Over and over again I've seen Reiki therapists become too enmeshed or entwined with their clients, with the results being stepping over boundaries, including sexual ones. When a person is trusting you to hold space for them to receive divine healing energy and grace that is all your role entails.

When you are in a healing practice, and a person seeks you out for assistance with a life issue, it is not your place to go out with them at night or become friends. While in a therapeutic relation-ship, you are in a powerful role to hold sacred space and channel healing energies.

Know too that people who come to you for healing can shine a light on issues or patterns you carry through life that require healing as well. You will be more compassionate as you 'get' how it feels for them, yet your experiences are often not helpful for your client to hear or know about then. They are there to seek assistance through you, not to be a sounding board for your issues.

Confidentiality means that whatever the person tells you regarding their experience, their life, or challenges are meant for your ears only. Far too often I've observed healers out in groups in coffee shops or restaurants chatting about people they have seen, using their names and identifying information in public! Sometimes, it has even sounded like gossip. Never do this! You are given an incredibly powerful role in holding sacred space for that person, and their healing process must be fuelled by unwavering privacy and trust.

6. **Shield Your Energy:** Reiki provides you with a shield of energy when working with other people. To work as expansively as you can with others, you also need to be very conscious about shielding yourself and your energy at all times; whether you are providing a healing session, out at an event or in any public space. When you are attuned to Reiki, and especially as a Reiki Master, you have an incredible light shining from within, and there are others in this world who will try to take advantage.

Find tools, including crystals infused with Reiki that protect your energy. Call on your Guides, Angels, and Archangels for help. I find surrounding myself with impenetrable gold light extending from below my feet to above my head allows me to move through the day and bounce off any energies trying to interfere with mine.

7. **Continually Do Your Healing:** I've consistently observed over twenty years of teaching that people attracted to this work often come from a place of being wounded or feeling like they don't fit in life. Sometimes, these wounds are more easily identifiable, as they may stem from experiencing or witnessing abuse, assault, or addiction. Know too that some wounds may not be as obvious nor

identified, such as neglect, family dynamic issues, chronic stress and challenges in quality of life.

> *People do not often address their overt or covert wounds unless they are causing a serious imbalance in their life. To be a great healer, you must continually excavate yourself, encouraging issues to rise to the surface and be in your awareness. Reiki, especially with crystals, will heal issues at the root cause.*

An unhealed wound leaves a place within you where energy cannot flow clearly, and allows fears to remain. One of the greatest qualities of Reiki is that you do not need to be consciously aware of those blockages to begin healing and releasing their energetic impact on you. Having the intention of healing them at the root cause releases them as much as possible at that particular point in time.

Accept that there are times for us as healers to seek out someone who has healed before and who works professionally with what is coming up for you in your life. Never feel ashamed about this need – ever. To grow and expand means that your wounds or issues will come to the surface for the light, healing and release. The more you support yourself in your continual healing and include ways in your life to do this on a regular basis, the stronger you will become as a healer. Through this, you will be given more energy, a higher vibration, and more powerful ability to assist others.

Developing Self-Awareness

Developing great self-awareness is a foundational element of being a great healer. The best healers are the ones who are continually aware of the power of what they do and say, accepting how their thoughts and actions impact the lives of those around them and their own. Great healers make choices based on what is optimal for the person who has come to them for assistance.

Self-awareness is knowing where you end, and the other person begins. It is about being the ultimate observer who can see within herself or himself and observe interactions with others with a higher vision and consciousness.

Having self-awareness does not mean that you see every client issue as it relates to you. It is about recognizing what are your issues and keeping them out of the therapeutic relationship. Awareness of what you require physically, mentally, emotionally, and spiritually involves checking in with yourself on a regular basis and listening to what you hear. Doing this is essential to being a powerful conduit of energies for healing and expansion.

Part III

Activating the Crystal Kingdom through the Reiki and Crystals Frequency

The Top Ten Crystals
to Use with Reiki

With the use of crystals or stones with Reiki, you are provided with advanced knowledge and energy that comes through the alignment of the two. Exploring each of these Top Ten Crystals with Reiki takes you on a journey to new dimensions of healing, expansion, and conscious awareness. Those included in this fundamental list came to me through extensive healing, teaching, direction and guidance. This list forms the foundation for what you require for healing, channeling, clearing energy, manifesting, expansion and strengthening with Reiki and Crystals.

Now, some of these stones may not be what others would consider their Top Ten. The reasons that these are in the Top Ten are:

1. Once a crystal is attuned and aligned with the Reiki and Crystal Frequency, its base purpose evolves and expands.

2. When activated with Reiki, those on this list become something new. Their purpose and abilities are much higher than without the Frequency of Reiki energy working in and through them.

This basic Top Ten List will also provide you with a comprehensive package of tools in working with crystal energy and stones for yourself and others. This Top Ten List covers all the bases in what people require to receive healing and expanding energies through you. Also, these Top Ten are relatively easy to find and very cost effective. You'll gain:

1. **Specific information about each crystal on the list:** For each crystal you will learn its properties, knowing that what you read here is not exhaustive. It is simply a starting point for you to continue your education with the knowledge of each stone. After working with crystals and stones for 20 years or more, I often feel as though I am just beginning and that there is so much to learn. Over and again, I've found having this great foundation is a necessity. Again, the favorite resource for people learning the basic information about crystals and stones is the *Crystal Bible*, especially Volumes One and Two.

2. **Strategies to use Reiki and Crystals Together:** You will find many ways to bring the powerful Reiki and Crystals Frequency into your work and life through the crystals you use. Always trust yourself and this process, keeping your intuition open, while having knowledge of a particular stone in your awareness. You'll gain great benefit from the Healing Spreads for each chakra.

3. **Energetically Empowered Messages:** Two great Ascended Masters, one being Merlin, and the other Hildegard of Bingen, channeled messages through me about each Crystal with Reiki, which are shared with you. There are further explanations of who they on upcoming pages.

4. **Learning about Unique Energies and Properties:** You've already learned about the new frequency coming through Reiki and Crystals together. Present in these words I write is energy to help align you with this unique frequency. Light and Healing Codes embedded here are turning on the Reiki and Crystal healing ability through you. The more you work with and meditate on these words, the stronger the energy will become in you.

5. **Crystal Spreads:** Using these stones, I've channeled (and tested) a Reiki and Crystal Healing Spread for each chakra. Using each spread on its corresponding chakra provides the optimal healing for the person you are assisting.

Meet Your Top Ten

You will find that these stones have a great impact on physical, mental, emotional, and spiritual levels. Their vibration conducts and works with the Reiki and Crystal Frequency in an optimal, consistent and energetically safe manner. Using the Reiki and Crystal Frequency will rapidly expand your ability to hold new light and energy while releasing old blockages, trauma, and pain at the root cause. For these basic Top Ten Crystals, here are the properties they have in common:

- Ease of use and consistency in effectiveness

- Readily available and reasonably priced

- Smaller, good quality pieces are equally as effective as larger ones

- Cleansing is simple, and for some not needed at all

- These stones readily channel the Reiki energies and move you and your client's experience to a much higher dimension

In no particular order, the Top Ten basic crystals to use with Reiki are:

1. Calcite

2. Amethyst

3. Clear Quartz

4. Tourmaline

5. Selenite

6. Kyanite

7. Tiger Eye

8. Rose Quartz

9. Jasper

10. Aqua Aura

Bonus: Ascended Master Assistance

As I began this book, the sense of divine guidance from the Ascended Master level became a constant, bringing in a very high vibration as I wrote. Ascended Masters represent fields of spiritual consciousness and knowledge. Their purpose is to guide and educate us in our process of rapid evolution and spiritual expansion. They may or may not have lived on Earth. From beyond the veil, they are unwavering pillars of strength, most easily accessible by those on a spiritual journey dedicated to opening to higher vibrations and living their soul purposes.

The two Ascended Masters who are assisting with the delivery of this new Frequency of Reiki and Crystals to you are Hildegard of Bingen and Merlin. Both have been constants with me on this path and I am forever grateful. Hildegard holds the field of knowledge of Earth energies and power of channeling. Merlin holds the field and knowledge of alchemy. Both of these – Earth energies and alchemy – are the essential forces comprising the Reiki and Crystals Frequency. Let's meet these Ascended Masters now.

Hildegard of Bingen

Living from the years 1098 to 1179, she was the tenth child in a wealthy Catholic family in Germany. At that time, the tenth child was committed to religious service. At a young age, Hildegard was placed in isolation with a widow named Jutta, who provided her with a foundation in religious teachings, music, and healing. At age 15, she joined her religious order and at age 38 she attained the distinction of the Abbess of their community. Through much conflict, she was able to secure independence and establish her nuns with their own community.

Throughout her life, Hildegard received religious visions that at times would leave her exhausted. In marathon sessions, she would channel with her scribe recording all that came through her. She left volumes of theology, information on healing, and magnificent music – still available today. Her book *Physika* contained information on healing, including the properties and uses of gemstones. Her list included emerald, onyx, beryl, topaz, jasper, amethyst, agate, pearls and diamond.

Merlin

People often only think of Merlin as a mythical character in the 6th-century British legend of King Arthur and Camelot. He did incarnate at that time, and also had further incarnations, including being Saint-Germain in the nineteenth century. He is a powerful teacher presence, holding the morphic field of alchemical knowledge and ability.

Merlin has been a powerful constant Guide on my journey, often making his presence known when I am challenged by rapid spiritual expansion and new knowledge. Connecting with his essence as I write this, I sense the profound alchemy of Reiki and Crystals. Among us, he is strongly present today, guiding us to own the wizardry and potential for personal transformation within and to anchor love and light on our planet.

Here are the Top Ten Crystals for you to work with the Reiki and Crystals Frequency:

#1 Calcite

Calcite works to heal the body's structural systems. When used with Reiki, the energy goes directly to the root of where required and simultaneously relieves and heals the problem while strengthening the system. Calcite is very good at pain reduction in the bones and joints. On an emotional level, it leaches out the fear often stored in hip and knee joints.

Calcite brings peace and calm and encourages a person to forgive others – as well as self. It is especially helpful on the physical, mental, emotional, and spiritual levels for people with degenerative issues. It assists to reduce the progression of the illness. Calcite can prepare a person's energy field for surgery and accelerated healing. It is particularly helpful for people undergoing and recovering from chemo-therapy treatment. Calcite is excellent for grounding when placed between feet. Here is one type of Calcite:

> *Pink Magnesium Calcite is sometimes called the "Reiki Stone." It has a gentle but powerful energy and is an excellent complement to energy healing modalities such as Reiki because of its excellent properties of energy magnification. It is a calming stone, which eases and heals the heart chakra. It fills the heart with universal love and self-love. It offers hope for the best. It heals inner child hurts and past abuse by filling one with a sense of motherly love. It is also*

excellent for channeling and astral travel, and for studying and retaining information learned.

~ from http://www.crystalsandjewelry.com

Here are a few specific types of Calcite that are especially effective when used with Reiki:

Red Calcite:

◎ Strengthens and heals the root chakra

◎ Stimulates the chakras behind the knees for help with confidence and moving out of a chronic pattern

◎ Strengthens the connection with the Earth consciousness

Orange Calcite:

◎ Powerful with hormonal and fertility issues for women, especially on the second chakra

◎ Clears emotions experienced as the result of trauma and past life issues

◎ Brings in the joy frequency and stimulates creativity

Calcite Message from Hildegard of Bingen

Calcite strengthens you as a Lightworker to move between dimensions, yet always returns you to your heart. It lightens your spirit by helping you be more playful and living in joy. You can move, fly and soar with your spirit yet

stay tethered to this earthly plane always to return home.
Chosen by us on a higher plane so you can visit with us
and remain in human form. With Calcite and Reiki, you
become shaman-like and bring multi-dimensional wisdom
and knowledge to the Earth. We thank you for this.

#2 Amethyst

If you could only have one crystal or stone to use with Reiki energies, it should be Amethyst. Of all the crystals I've worked with, Amethyst's natural energies best embody the essence of Reiki. What is amazing about Amethyst is that with Reiki and pure intention, you can use and program it to work on the physical, mental, emotional and spiritual levels in ways that recipients most optimally require. You can adapt this crystal to any situation or requirement and program it with Reiki to resonate and respond however needed. It's the chameleon of crystals with Reiki – it adapts its abilities and frequency to its surroundings and requirements.

Amethyst brings peace, tranquility and calm. The environment that it creates provides the foundation for optimal healing and expansion. Whatever you are addressing with Amethyst, its inherent loving nature directs it to the root cause with gentleness for healing and strengthening. The power of Amethyst can sometimes be so subtle that people negate its ability to enable shifts on all levels.

Amethyst is very multi-dimensional in nature. Historically, it has been deemed the royal stone, often worn to represent a great human connection with the Divine and for protection from outside forces. Wearing Amethyst and keeping it in your environment links you to higher vibrations and strengthens your chi.

Know the location of the source of your Amethyst. Particularly with Reiki and Amethyst, knowing the source location of the crystal will assist you in maximizing how and when you use it. You will soon have several Amethysts, and you'll come to know through practice that each has its uniqueness. The Amethyst from Thunder Bay, Canada connects you deeply with the Earth with very grounding aspects. Those from Brazil attract Earth devas and spirits and those from Uruguay align the receiver with the highest vibration that they can hold at that time. Here two specific types of Amethyst that are very powerful with the Reiki and Crystal Frequency:

Ametrine: This Amethyst and Citrine combination is its own crystal, not a form of Amethyst. When used with Reiki, Ametrine powerfully removes energetic blockages stopping a person from fully embracing who they are. Use in the heart chakra and kidney areas. Ametrine is great to use with Reiki for maximizing intention and manifesting.

Phantom Rove: It is one of my favorites with Reiki for healing at the cause of an issue. It is Amethyst with high levels of iron, so rather than being purple, it is a rust color. It is unique to Amethyst from the Thunder Bay, Ontario area. Phantom Rove activates the ability for your Guides to work with your client's Guides for the highest good. For people whose 'mental energy' is low (lethargy, low iron, experiencing grief), Phantom Rove with Reiki is the remedy.

Amethyst Message from Merlin

> *Amethyst invites you to the dance of healing and living a soul-based life. It is the best partner as it takes your hand, guides you forward and never steps on your feet. The presence of this stone and where it's located on this planet is not by chance. Moreover, its peaceful yet powerful vibration and limitless potential provide the user with protection and enlightened decision-making. It was given to leaders for the latter purpose. Ever on call, Amethyst energy will visit and work with you through the night strengthening*

your highest self and resolve. When charged with Reiki, it guides the Ascended Masters to your door, providing you with the opportunity to sit at their feet and learn from them.

#3 Clear Quartz Crystal

Clear Quartz is the most common family of crystals available to us and is found all over the world. It disguises itself by its simplicity – many people underestimate its qualities as it often looks so 'plain.' When you begin to explore the types of clear Quartz and its limitless properties and structural appearance, you learn how powerful Quartz is in both our earthly world and in accessing higher realms. As a Reiki practitioner, you will discover a few that remain your favorites over the years, developing a deep connection that cannot be logically understood.

> *Quartz is known as the Master Healing Crystal because it contains the full spectrum of light and as such will work on every level to bring the body into balance. It strengthens and stabilizes the body's energy fields and promotes harmony. Clear Quartz can amplify both positive thoughts and energy and can stimulate positive action when it is needed. Clear Quartz can.be used to harmonize all the chakras as it contains all the colors in the light spectrum.*
>
> *~ from http://www.crystalwellbeing.co.uk*

From my experience, Clear Quartz with Reiki works well on a systemic level. It clears blocks that inhibit the role of physical systems, such as the lymphatic or immune. It then activates the system to perform the function for which it is designed at a vibrant and optimal level. I've even used it to clear non-physical energy systems, such as family conflicts and organizational issues.

As there are many types of clear Quartz with many different properties, the level of their vibration can vary. Even with Reiki energies, some clear Quartz can only assist to a certain level. It's important to learn the type of Quartz and its properties that you are working with, especially as many can be of very high frequency. Be mindful using clear Quartz, especially higher vibrational stones. Herkimer Diamonds and Lemeurian Seed Crystals, for instance, can elevate and propel you or your client to a very high vibration when grounding and nurturing is required.

Clear Quartz Message from Hildegard

She walks like the sun stabilizing the Earth beneath your feet. Her purpose is being in service for others. She opens her heart for the Universe to sing through to you. The song changes with each quality she holds, yet it is always attuned to you with the vibrational frequency of love. Ever expanding, she can teach you for this and many lifetimes.

An entire book (or two) could be written about Quartz Crystals and their variety and unique purposes. Here is a noteworthy clear Quartz Crystal that is optimal for use with the Reiki and Crystals Frequency.

Herkimer Diamonds: These crystals have called to me and been a faithful power source since I began this work. Genuine Herkimer Diamonds come from Herkimer, New York. There are other Herkimer Diamonds in the marketplace now, so ask the origins of any you may purchase.

With Reiki, this crystal can penetrate through any interference or resistance to heal multi-dimensionally the source of an issue. Wearing this stone provides you with higher wisdom and accessible insights, especially when treating others. When you wear or use a Herkimer in combination with another crystal, the energy of the other is amplified, so be mindful of any combinations so that you are not overwhelmed. You'll find additional information for Herkimer Diamonds, as well as phantoms and inclusions found in Quartz Crystals under the Advanced Crystals for Channeling section later in this book.

#4 Tourmaline

Tourmaline is a powerful healing stone that links spiritual healing to physical matter. It comes in many colors, each with unique qualities and abilities. It pushes that which is deep and hidden to reveal itself, lighten energetically and move out.

Since Reiki has its own wisdom and works on the root cause of issues, partnering it with Tourmaline is very powerful. Often with clients, I visualize a bed of Tourmaline beneath my Reiki table when clearing this and past life blockages and dense energies. It gently moves the issues to the surface and lightly takes them away from the body while clearing both the person and their auric field of old energies and their effects.

Tourmaline is a very gentle and powerful crystal. When activated with the Reiki energy, small amounts of it can clear the chakras, body, and physical environment, and leave a sweet feeling of wellbeing. Tourmaline is also a protective stone, shielding you from both intentional and unintentional negativity trying to interfere with you.

In 2013, I received this message from Tourmaline and Reiki together. It shows how tourmaline's purpose is being transformed to assist with our need now:

> *My beauty has been seen since days of old. The Ancients knew how to ignite my abilities. Forgotten is that knowledge until now – Reiki brings me back to my full potential for you. With this new fire, my range for you is three-fold:*

1) within the Earth,
2) upon the Earth, and
3) in the heavens.

Within the Earth, my presence (and of course appeal) is nearly global. My role in the healing of this planet is 'stabilization', working with both the root chakra of people and the Earth. The Earth mother is receiving much interference now, and what humans are doing is only one aspect of this negative influence.

Use the darker-colored stones to meditate and connect with the power of my stabilizing presence. Use your intention to align with tourmaline beds within the Earth, asking to strengthen their interconnection for the planet while pulling up my energy for your 'stabilization' or grounding.

On the Earth, you receive balanced healing through me. When Reiki energy and symbols are added, my healing for you and others is powerful with a three-pronged ability. Place on or near the root, sacral or solar plexus chakra and place your hands over me. With Reiki, I can reach below to clear blockages and strengthen the body's core systems. Secondly, my ability to strengthen and heal your body now is profound – especially solar plexus concerns.

Thirdly, with Reiki, I provide a portal for 'groups' to address healing needs. Your prayers are being heard, and we come together for your healing and that of the Earth. Tourmaline with Reiki provides us the open door to come through. (*We refers to Earthly and Heavenly healers working together).

This third prong of Tourmaline and Reiki providing the portal for healing groups cannot be minimized. While writing this and having Black Tourmaline next to me, I feel the presence of many groups – choirs of angels, an assembly of ancient healers, including Merlin's frequency and my committee of Ascended Masters. They are ready to come through to assist us. Bring Tourmaline activated with Reiki into your healing and meditation sessions. (While writing this section, I am being told to state that Tourmaline with Reiki provides a protective experience only allowing what is for the highest good to come through).

Tourmaline Message from Merlin

> *During my many incarnations, I sought out this stone, often journeying to locate it. Once I did, it reminded me of what I knew in previous times, including my deep connection with the Ancient Ones and the Goddess. At times when despair and even physical pain tried to stop me, tourmaline brought me back to my senses and nudged me to carry on.*

As you have read, our spiritual Guides want you to know of the evolving, powerful purpose of Tourmaline. Here are more details about specific types of Tourmaline when used with Reiki.

Black Tourmaline (Schorl): One of my all-purpose favorites. When used with Reiki, Black Tourmaline powerfully:

- Clears physical, mental and emotional lower states (negativity) from the physical, mental, and emotional body

- Loosens chronic pain and relieves it

- Enables higher self to take charge

- Provides shielding from negative energies and interferences

Pink Tourmaline:

- Releases fear stuck in and around the heart chakra

- Heals and strengthens the heart chakra

- Expands manifesting ability

- Opens the ability to access the morphic field of all possibility

Red Tourmaline (Rubellite):

- Gently and rapidly accelerates healing of the physical heart and circulation

- Balances energy meridians

- Raises chi (life force) and increases energy

- Increases strength of the energy field of any organ that deals with blood or circulation

- Increases self-awareness

Green Tourmaline:

- Facilitates self-love

- Heals past trauma and post-traumatic stress

- Evolves spiritual consciousness

- Expands your awareness of God's love for you

- Opens channels for nurturing from the Earth

Watermelon Tourmaline:

- The smiling stone – you can't help but smile

- Strengthens your ability to feel the Frequency of Joy

- Reduces the roller coaster of emotional highs and lows

- Activates the chakra between the eyes (bridge of nose) to bring in a 'new vision'

- Anchors you in your new state of being following a shift in consciousness

Brown Tourmaline (Dravite):

- Repairs fragments in the psyche or sense of self

- Heals detrimental archetypical patterns

- Provides a sense of well-being during 'trials of initiation'

- Gives focus, determination and reinvigoration on the spiritual path

- Heals specific physical systems i.e. digestion, elimination, fascia

#5 Selenite

Selenite is an essential stone with Reiki and Crystals due to its versatility and high vibrational frequency. The vibration of the Selenite with Reiki is one of the most potent on this Top Ten list. Selenite fits perfectly with the G.R.A.G. model as it readily receives, generates, amplifies, and grounds new energies in the body. It is also an all purpose cleansing agent for other crystals and it does not require any cleansing itself.

In and of itself, it is a very high vibrational crystal that moves the user to higher realms of consciousness and energy. Meditating with Selenite will:

- Increase your ability to connect with your highest self

- Strengthen your intuition

- Open channels to receive messages and insights

- Activate dormant abilities within you

Often in my work, I use Selenite to raise the vibration of a group's energy by sending its energy to a class or speaking engagement before it is scheduled to occur. Selenite constantly assists as a catalyst for accessing and channeling higher frequencies and in raising and solidifying a person's frequency in a higher dimension (as with the 5th Dimensional Consciousness program). One of my primary tools is an 18-inch Selenite wand that I use with the Reiki technique of Byosen scanning rather than my hands. I find that it not only provides me information through the scan, it also opens the etheric body and begins the healing process immediately.

Selenite must be highly respected and honored. It is very easy to be overwhelmed and ungrounded when working with Selenite with Reiki as it opens the higher chakras very rapidly. (People who sleep with Selenite in their bedroom often report sleep disruptions). Use Selenite strategically and build your relationship with it. When beginning to work with it in meditation, keep it on the floor below you and not in direct contact with your body.

Selenite is also an amazing energy filter in a room – an essential for your Reiki healing space. A pillar-shaped piece infused with Reiki symbols is optimal. It will happily chug along, clearing as you go. To cleanse other crystals, I place crystals on a large Selenite bar immediately after use. Within a couple of hours, the crystals are cleansed and recharged.

Selenite Message from Merlin

Selenite says: "Light consciousness and the breath of life flows through me. I hold up the Earth vibration of the planet intertwining the male and female for flexible elastic movement and willingness to let the other lead when required." Selenite with Reiki is the power to clear away the past for a bright future for the planet. Through Selenite runs the vibration of the Earth and her healing wisdom and strength. Selenite connects you with Source Energy moving through your Crown to your heart energy. Its beauty knows no bounds, especially with intention. Selenite anchors you in a state of grace and abundant living. It is the God-consciousness made real in Earth form and allows you to have insight into the mind of God.

#6 Kyanite

From the same family as Selenite, Kyanite is a powerful healer's stone. It is very versatile in nature and is most often light blue in color. Light blue is the color associated with the energy of Mother Mary (who embodies Divine Feminine energy). Kyanite assists you in accessing higher states of awareness, dreaming and protects your energy. It does not require cleansing as it cannot hold negative emotions, which makes it optimal to keep on you when wanting to shield your energy from interferences.

Kyanite is most in its element when used with Reiki for clearing emotional and core imbalances in the body. When a person is experiencing uncomfortable emotions, Kyanite goes to work, leaching the angst from a person's body and leaving in its place a sense of deep nurturing, peace and rejuvenation. Place one piece in each hand of the person requesting emotional healing or in crisis. When a person is overwhelmed by their emotions, placing Kyanite between the knees is very helpful. Additional help comes through when placed over the heart chakra. Though most blue stones work with the Throat Chakra energies; when working with Reiki and Kyanite, I don't often find myself placing Kyanite in that area.

Kyanite never needs cleansing. Here are three specific types of Kyanite that excel when used with Reiki:

Blue Kyanite: An all-around energy enhancer that works very quickly to removes blockages in the aura and chakra system. All kyanite increase the connection between the disparate aspects of self. It also aligns the human form with the astral plane. Blue kyanite stimulates the third eye and psychic abilities, connecting to Spirit Guides and Guardians. Kyanite enhances dreamwork and astral travel. It works on the entire chakra system and integrates the physical and etheric bodies. It also balances male and female energies and encourages them to grow together.

Black Kyanite: Simultaneously improves grounding and increases energy, Black Kyanite offers protection from negative influence. It works effectively on the physical body and helps to center the consciousness in the body and assists with meditation and focus.

Green Kyanite: With Reiki, Green Kyanite releases at the root cause fear, pain and hurt from this and past lifetimes with gentleness and precision. It opens the heart chakra and connects you to the truth of the heart. Green Kyanite relates to the flowing, dynamic energy of nature. It connects you to the inner emotional landscape and assists in creating new emotional pathways.

Kyanite Message from Merlin

> *Kyanite brings a new rhythm to your life. Your Earth is being challenged in its battle of light and lighter and dark and heavier in the Fourth Dimension. Loved ones, Kyanite, is a gift for you. It clears you from the fallout from forces out of your awareness and influence. With Reiki, it leaches the unwanted from your body and eliminates that which undoes you on a third-dimensional plane. Daily use will keep you clear and balance all your meridians, allowing light energy to flow through you.*

#7 Tiger Eye

A late-comer to this Top Ten list of Crystals with Reiki, Tiger Eye revealed its powerful self to me over time. The awareness of its power came through observation and recognition of how diligently it thoroughly healed without fanfare. Tiger Eye is like that person in a group who seldom speaks, yet when they do, everyone listens.

Tiger Eye with Reiki is the embodiment of the sacred masculine. It archetypically represents male qualities often discounted in living a soul-based life. These qualities include focus, discernment, logic, reason, steadfastness, perseverance and assertiveness (not aggression).

Tiger Eye is optimal when chosen for wearing or healing in an intentional way. Not meant to be continually worn by lightworkers, it is optimal for healers and shamans to wear after an intensive healing session or to assist in returning to the here and now when too long in another dimension. Tiger Eye assists with lung issues, and when used with Reiki enables the user to breathe in the sweetness of life. Tiger Eye is also especially helpful with the solar plexus. I've used it consistently with Reiki for women who are a) healing from being victimized, and b) learning to recognize, hold, and use their power. In addition, here are two powerful stones:

Tiger Iron: This combination of Tiger Eye and Hematite (iron) is fabulous when a person has any blood, circulation or hormonal issues, especially when placed over the liver.

Blue Tiger Eye: This stone jumped out at me in a small crystal shop in Cardiff, Wales. It holds such a powerful, low-key energy. Great with Reiki for communication, meetings and planning events. Hold Blue Tiger Eye while focusing on the Reiki symbol Hen Shaze Shonen and sending energy to a future event.

Tiger Eye Message from Merlin

(As I begin to scribe this message from Merlin, I saw him surrounded by his male peers). We Ancients knew the power of Tiger Eye and revered it above most others. It gives the ability to bend time and move through dimensions. Your planet requires its indefatigable spirit and should be the touchstone for all Warriors of the Light.

Those in earthly power will be drawn to it now without consciously knowing that it is calling to them. Choosing it brings consistency and power. Choose it now as a keystone for you on your soul journey.

#8 Rose Quartz

There is a smile on my face as I begin to write about this crystal. Next to Amethyst, Rose Quartz is one of the most versatile in this TopTen List. All emotional healing and transformation accelerate. A person's connection with self plus enhanced self-esteem and self-awareness rapidly occurs. Rose Quartz – especially when used in conjunction with Reiki – releases us from old patterns, thought forms, core beliefs about self and opens us to new, higher vibrations and love. Forgiving yourself and others becomes much easier. It is especially helpful for people experiencing and healing post-traumatic stress or mental health issues.

Rose Quartz is helpful on the heart chakra as well as the Sacral Chakra (especially with any reproductive issues in women). Placing a flat piece under a person's heart chakra before laying down for their treatment and one on top of this chakra, then placing your hands over the Heart Chakra during the treatment, provides a person with deep healing and nurturing in a very gentle manner. It is rare for Rose Quartz to overwhelm a person, so use it with people who feel fragile, emotionally vulnerable, or in crisis.

Reiki and Rose Quartz open a portal enabling divine feminine energy to enter the healing or meditation experience. Through this portal, the Frequency of Love can channel. Often with Rose Quartz and Reiki, the presence and healing power of female Ascended Masters enters and encircles the experience with profound sacredness. This State of Grace provides the optimal environment for Reiki miracles to occur.

Pink is not a color usually associated with power. People perceive pink as a color of gentleness, passivity, and calm – attributes that are not usually given high value in a fear-based world. Rose Quartz, with its various depths of pink, from pale to lavender, is one of the most powerful stones available to us, especially when activated with Reiki. Connect with these four powerful features of Rose Quartz with Reiki:

1. Reiki brings out the warrior qualities often hidden in Rose Quartz. Being a warrior means to have focus, unwavering determination, strength, and compassion. A warrior utilizes all of her or his resources to go to the depth of an issue and 'leaves no stone unturned' when it comes to creating solutions. This is the energy of Reiki and Rose Quartz together.

2. When activating Rose Quartz with Reiki, especially over the heart chakra, fears rapidly melt away. This process goes to the root of current-life or past-life issues, especially when you intend for them to do so. For anyone who has experienced trauma and lives with post-traumatic symptoms, Reiki with Rose Quartz clears fear at the cellular level.

3. Rose Quartz provides the user with a sense of well-being and a greater ability to give and receive love. When Rose Quartz is activated with Reiki, the ability for a person to access a higher experience of love is increased tenfold, if not more. One of the light frequencies readily available to us as humans is that of the 'Frequency of Love.' We instinctually know that this higher love is available for us to experience, yet on a day-to-day basis people continually search for it and often confuse it with 'romantic love.' When a person meditates with Rose Quartz infused with Reiki and the intention to have this 'higher love' flow through, a door opens. You experience the feeling of how we are meant to live each day.

Every crystal on this Top Ten list brings you a special message. My awareness of the Rose Quartz message took me by surprise, as it arrived while I was sitting in a coffee shop reviewing my schedule. Not surprising that sitting directly in front of me were two college-age women planning a community fundraiser, to the left of me a mother with a baby (in a bright pink snowsuit), and to my right, two beautiful grandmothers speaking lovingly about their grandchildren. Demonstrated by this is the beauty of the divine feminine all around us – the Maiden, the Mother, and the Crone – even in the oddest of places.

Rose Quartz Message through Hildegard of Bingen

My presence and influence have been consistent since the consciousness of this planet began. (I am one of the original energy keepers placed here). You may often pass over me for one who speaks more loudly to you. I am the source for the healing, nurturing and direction you crave.

Through me, the divine feminine and her many faces are gifted to you. See the many faces and all the aspects of feminine power and influence – not only what you've been taught to believe about women's power. Through me comes the source energy from Isis, the compassion of Quan Yin, the powerful mothering of Mary, the oneness of all vision of White Buffalo Calf Woman and the warrior embodied by Maeve. You can call on me for limitless power, strength and wisdom beyond what you have ever experienced in your physical form.

The morphic field of Rose Quartz energy is being reactivated and expanded. This gentle bringer of nurturing and mother energy will soon be elevated to the most powerful stone on our planet. The realignment and re-anchoring of the Mary Frequency will become complete in the year 2052. Rose Quartz frees you from chaos and uncertainty, revealing to you the power of gentleness and providing the fuel for stepping up. Rose Quartz and Reiki elevates you through the times when loving is a challenge. It brings you the guidance, strength, resolve, power and wisdom to persevere from the heart. Rose Quartz says, "I've been sitting in the corner for a long, long time, and now I am stepping into the Light."

#9 Jasper

Jasper is like a warm seat by the fire, wrapped in a blanket on a cold winter's night. It is always a gentle, nurturing powerhouse. The availability, types and healing properties of Jasper with Reiki are incredibly varied and include:

✓ Rapid grounding and energizing the legs and feet

✓ Healing the lower three chakras

✓ Being rooted with the Earth

✓ Receiving information from the Earth Consciousness

✓ Energizing areas of deficit in the body systems and organs, especially in the first three chakra regions

✓ Shielding the energetic body from negative energy

✓ Healing and supporting the endocrine system and functioning

When Reiki infuses Jasper, it is like taking a wallflower and making them the life of the party. Jasper is incredibly powerful, yet often ignored as it is deeply intelligent and loving, yet quiet and ego-free. Infusing Jasper with Reiki allows its magical properties and innate intelligence to flow. Great healing occurs as its impact expands layer after layer in the physical, mental, emotional and spiritual body until the job is complete. Jasper is also easy to wear, and I often carry a piece in each hip pocket. Though best worn directly on the skin, having Jasper anywhere on your body provides you with a constant, supportive, wise friend that never overwhelms. Some of the most optimal types of Jasper to use with Reiki are:

Red Jasper:

- Immediately provides a sense of well-being, safety and relaxation

- Energizes the legs, balancing their meridians, increasing energy flow and the ability for self-support

- Releases fear often held in the knees

- Stimulates the chakras in the knees, assisting a person to move forward

Yellow Jasper:

- Heals, strengthens, and detoxes the organs of the solar-plexus area (liver, gall bladder, stomach, pancreas, and spleen)

- Quickly strengthens the Solar Plexus chakra, the power center of the body

- Enables greater self-esteem and confidence

○ Healing with traumatic issues, especially the impact of physical and sexual assault

Picture Jasper:

○ Provides a pulsating beacon of love to the body and spirit

○ Clarifies past life information being received

○ Supports and strengths Spirit in the physical body

Ocean Jasper:

○ Though not from the ocean, it brings in the healing power and knowledge from the seas

○ Reduces stress with deep, calm and gentle floating experiences

Jasper Message through Merlin

> Jasper says, "My wisdom goes before time immortal. The Ancients held me up and gave me as a gift for strengthening the human form." Jasper speaks of coming in many colors and patterns, yet its core vibration is that of the deepest green of the magical forest – earthy, earthy, earthy. Jasper is ready to reveal itself to those who ask, ready to do battle for you and ready to keep you company on the coldest of nights. Keep Jasper close to you as a constant, unwavering and steady friend always bringing you back to the home in yourself.

#10 Aqua Aura

Though this unique stone may not be on the usual Top Ten list for crystal healing, it is considered an essential stone for healing with the Reiki and Crystals Frequency. Aqua Aura does not come directly from the Earth for our use and is created this way:

> *Aqua aura is Quartz that is gold infused by taking 12 hours to heat the Quartz to 1600F while setting a vacuum equal to 2 earth atmospheres, then letting chemically purified gold vapors into the chamber when the temperature and vacuum are correct. This bonds the gold to the lattice of the crystal, forming a permanent bond to the surface of the Quartz and giving it an electric blue color.*
>
> ~ *www.celestialights.com*

The outcomes of working with Aqua Aura in healing include greater intuition, an increase in psychic abilities, deeper meditation, moments of enlightened self-knowledge and higher wisdom. It is a great tool for pulling Light into the body and releasing or removing low-vibration energies from the body. It is especially powerful with the Throat Chakra.

Many people come to and continue to study Reiki as it speaks to their own inherent alchemical nature. An alchemist is a wizard who specializes in the process of transmutation (a higher spiritual experience than transformation). Traditionally, we define alchemy as being ability to turn lead into gold. Aqua Aura with Reiki works in the realms of wizardry and limitless possibility here on Earth.

Aqua Aura Message from Hildegard

We showed those who created her how to do it. Aqua Aura is not meant to be hidden or contained. Her brilliance parallels the Light within you, attuning your throat to sing her song of healing from the highest vibration. She is alchemy and brings out the Creator in you. With her, you will think new thoughts, dream new dreams, and become a visionary with feet firmly planted on the ground. Though she is new to the planet, she provides information from the Ancient Ones with healing from the oceans and the skies. Treat her with respect. Allow yourself to grow with her and, at times, take a rest from her as well.

Now that you have met the Top Ten Crystals, let's move on to how to specifically use them for healing and expansion.

Crystals, Reiki, and the Chakras

If you have been exploring crystals as tools for healing before reading this book, you may have already found and used elaborate spreads of crystals placed on or around the body for healing and expansion. Often, people become overwhelmed when reading the directions for these and the amount and variety of stones required. Activating the Reiki and Crystals Frequency allows you to facilitate healing and expansion on the physical, mental, emotional, and spiritual level in a very simple, direct and profound manner.

Much of traditional crystal healing requires you to have many crystals, and larger ones as well. The time and financial investment to secure them can be great. With the Reiki and Crystal Frequency, you can focus on smaller, more reasonably priced stones, as with the Top Ten you've already met. With this approach, healing and spiritual expansion are focused in a laser-like manner, using a proven system with great time management and cost effectiveness built in. Here are the most powerful outcomes of this new approach:

- Healing the physical, mental, emotional and spiritual body simultaneously

- Greater intention and focus combined with stronger intuitive knowing

- Strengthening and healing individual chakras, and how they work together

⊚ Providing energy for the entire chakra system

⊚ Activating a particular energy center's ability to raise the body's vibration

⊚ Expanding the power of the seven major and smaller minor energy centers to fulfill their highest purposes

⊚ Enabling root cause healing of current and past life issues and for future requirements

⊚ Opening channels for divine intervention at the highest levels

⊚ Activate Earth connections enabling deep grounding

The Chakra System

Through your Reiki learning, you`ve learned about the chakra system. Chakras and their vitality are the real foundations of health and spiritual expansion for all living beings. Most western teachings refer to the seven chakras in the body, and some systems include the five above the head. Over the past few years, I've intensely explored and taught the chakra centers below our bodies that extend into the Earth – but that is for another book. For now, we'll focus on the seven chakras in the body and reference the ones above the Crown and below the Root chakras.

> *One of the greatest false beliefs that students of spirituality hold is that the upper chakras (Third Eye and Crown) are more important or valuable than the lower chakras (Sacral and Root). Wrong, wrong, wrong. The chakra system is*

interconnected. If the lower chakras are weak, you cannot
expand the abilities and potential of your Highest Self.

Here is a summary for reference for each of the seven chakras. Later, you'll find a chart suggesting the optional crystals to use with each chakra.

Chakra One – Root Chakra: Centered between the genitals and the anus, the Root provides a physical connection with the Earth. Energetically, it points to the Earth, allowing energy to move up from it and down from the body. Everything in life rests on and builds from the strength of the Root Chakra. People are tribal by nature, and your ability to form bonds with others rests here. The effectiveness of how you meet the requirements of life such as food, shelter, finances, sexual functioning and self-care rests here. If you have chronic financial or relationship issues, work on your Root.

Chakra Two – Sacral Chakra: It is located in the lower abdomen between the pubic bone and the navel at the front and back of the body. (Chakras Two to Six are centered in the body and expand out the front and the back). As the Root Chakra is about primal functioning, the Sacral Chakra is about the quality of that functioning. With a strong Sacral Chakra, you have healthier relationships, sensual experiences, feel abundance, experience emotions and move more fluidly through life. Often overlooked are two higher life functions that reside here: intuition and creative ability.

Chakra Three – Solar Plexus: Your power center resides here. Power is not about control or dominance over others. Power is about how effectively you remain in your core of self and use strength and tools while life challenges and dramas swirl around you. Residing here is your sense of self and ability to overcome patterns of behavior and beliefs that no longer serve you. The energy to make choices and decisions that are for the highest good comes from a strong Solar Plexus Chakra.

Chakra Four – The Heart: The Heart Chakra is about your ability to give and receive love. It is in the middle of the seven chakra system. The Heart Chakra processes the information from the upper three and the lower three chakras for your highest good. The Heart is meant to be in charge of your body – not the mind. It is also the entrance to the Field of All Possibility. All Lightworkers need to be committed to healing, removing and releasing all held fear that congeals around the Heart Chakra and strangles its potential.

Chakra Five – Throat Chakra: The first of the upper three chakras, the Throat Chakra is about the refinement of the self as reflected through the genuineness and focus of self-expression. It is your center of communication – both expression and listening. (Now with limitless communication globally, people are speaking yet few are listening, which is allowing heavier, more toxic energies to dominate). Be an observer of what you say, how you say it and how you listen to strengthen this powerful chakra.

Chakra Six – Third Eye: This Chakra is also known as the Brow Chakra. Often people believe that opening this center will rapidly expand spiritual consciousness. That can happen, but when 'forced' by overloading it with crystals, a person can experience physical symptoms and a roller-coaster of emotions. With the Reiki and Crystal Frequency, this can even worsen.

The goal is to strengthen and expand the Third Eye Center while doing the same with the rest of the chakras. To live multi-dimensionally, higher vision and cosmic connection needs to be held and supported by a firm foundation of energetic strength provided by the lower three chakras.

Chakra Seven – The Crown: As the Root Chakra points downward, the Crown points upward connecting with Source energy. The purpose of the Crown Chakra is a connection with the Divine, including the ability to access universal knowledge and our timeless nature. Reiki has been said to provide us with the keys to Heaven on Earth. The Crown Chakra provides the portal where Reiki energies flow into us.

Chakra Strengthening with Reiki and Crystals

This section will provide you with the tools and techniques for healing, balancing, and expansion of specific chakras using the Reiki and Crystal Frequency. Unique to this system is how all three – healing, balancing and expansion – occur simultaneously. You'll learn to give:

1.   A full-body, chakra-based treatment, and

2.   Chakra specific intensive healing and light activations.

If you've already acquired the Top Ten Crystals for working with Reiki, you already have all you need to complete the spread on the body for yourself or others.

The following chart suggests crystals to use with each chakra. The intention is that these are relatively easy to find, cost-effective, and you can get big results from a small stone.

Seventh Chakra:	amethyst, clear quartz (small stone),
Crown	tourmaline, lepidolite, celestite, blue
Chakra Color:	sapphire (Note: placed next to the
Violet, White	head without touching near the body).

Sixth Chakra:
Third Eye
Chakra Color:
Indigo, White

amethyst, rose quartz, kunzite (small piece), clear quartz (small piece), sodalite, lapis lazuli (Note: placed next to head near Third Eye without touching).

Fifth Chakra:
Throat
Chakra Color:
Sky Blue, Turquoise

aqua aura, turquoise, chrysocolla, blue calcite, lapis lazuli, sodalite, blue kyanite, azurite, chrysoprase, pearl, aquamarine, chalcedony

Fourth Chakra:
Heart
Chakra Color:
Green, Pink, White

rose quartz, selenite, kyanite (especially green), moss agate, seraphinite, labradorite, rhodochrosite, olivine, aventurine, fluorite

Third Chakra:
Solar Plexus
Chakra Color:
Yellow

calcite, selenite, citrine, clear quartz (needs to be programmed), yellow jasper, chrysocolla, tiger eye (especially for men), yellow tourmaline

Second Chakra:
Sacral
Chakra Color:
Orange

orange or yellow calcite, carnelian, orange or ocean jasper, rhodochrosite, amethyst

First Chakra:
Root
Chakra Color:
Red

red jasper (mookite), malachite, darker amethyst, phantom rove (amethyst with iron from Canada), smoky quartz, red coral, cinnabar, tiger eye (especially for men), garnet, carnelian, black tourmaline

Tips for Crystal Placement

1. For Crown and Third Eye, do not place crystals directly on the body. For Crown, place one to three inches away from the top of the head. For Third Eye, place one to three inches either left or right of the eyes.

2. If a crystal moves, slips or rolls away, do not be concerned. It will end up exactly where required for the healing session.

3. Place the crystals in order, starting at the root chakra and moving to the head. Remove the crystals slowly and gently starting at the head and finishing with the root chakra.

4. Avoid black stones as they may counteract the benefits of the treatment.

The Basic Full-Body Spread

Balance does not mean a perfect evenness. Balance means bringing back to center the energies of a chakra. Being balanced in this way is the first step to strengthening each chakra, rapidly accelerating healing in the energy body which, in turn, improves the physical, mental and emotional bodies and lays the foundation for spiritual expansion.

This basic spread is a great overall tonic for yourself or your client. You'll choose just one crystal for each chakra. The temptation may be to use multiple stones on each chakra or higher vibration stones (e.g. phenacite, lemurian seed crystals) on the upper chakras. Avoid doing this! It is easy to overstimulate a person, undo healing and make things worse. You can also add one or two additional stones to address a specific issue, such as placing calcite on a painful joint.

Use the preceding reference chart or use your Energy-testing skills to choose the optimal crystal. If you do not have the color or type of stone suggested for each chakra, then use the most similar stone you have. You'll place that crystal over or near the chakra while providing a full body treatment. For yourself, do this laying down. Never worry if a crystal moves or shifts as it knows where to go!

Before you start, do Reiki with the crystals, adding any intentions for programming and symbols. Place the crystals and apply Reiki directly on, or over each chakra. It is suggested to place a larger, grounding stone between the feet. Here are the directions for the Full-Body Spread as provided on a Reiki table:

To Begin: No crystals. Sit or stand above the recipients head, with your hands on their shoulders. Say a silent prayer, asking for the Reiki and Crystal Frequency to be activated. Place your intention in your Heart Chakra, listening from here for what their body is communicating to you. Minimum five minutes.

For the Active Full-Body Spread: Place the pre-chosen crystal for each chakra on or near it. For the Third Eye and Crown, the crystal is placed next to, and not on the head. Provide a full-body treatment, either in the order for Usui hand positions or as you are intuitively guided. Minimum 15 minutes.

To Finish: Remove crystals starting with the Crown and remove in order towards the Root. Keep the stone between the feet, and place your hands on the feet for a minimum three minutes, with the intention for grounding and sealing in the healing energy for the client. Give a silent Prayer of Thanks.

Advanced Chakra Specific Healing and Expansion Spreads

The creation of these Chakra Healing and Expansion Spreads is the combination of divine guidance and earthly experience. A 'spread' is a combination of chakra specific stones, placed in a pattern and activated with the Reiki and Crystal Frequency. You know that the Chakra system is the foundational energy system in the body, and when a chakra is depleted or underfunctioning, then physical, mental, emotional or spiritual issues arise in the body. These issues can appear in the area of a specific chakra or be systemic. Through experience and observation, the following occurs when these advanced spreads are activated:

⑤ Deep and thorough healing of current life issues at the root cause

⑤ Connection with and clearing of past-life issues that impact the present Healing of the specific chakra, so any deficits are healed and full functioning restored

⑤ Improvement of the energy flowing between chakras

⑤ Expansion of a person's limitless potential due to the release of deep blockages, beliefs, and energetic interferences

The following contains the directions for the crystal spread for each chakra, with a photo to assist you. You'll see some suggestions for crystals to use with each, and also refer to the preceding chart and other resources on crystal information. Trust your inner knowing and spiritual guidance and you'll be amazed at the results!

#1 Root Chakra Spread

✓ Alleviation of pain in region

✓ Grounding, increasing mental focus and ability to manage energy

✓ Issues related to basic requirements of life – food, shelter, clothing, family ties, finances

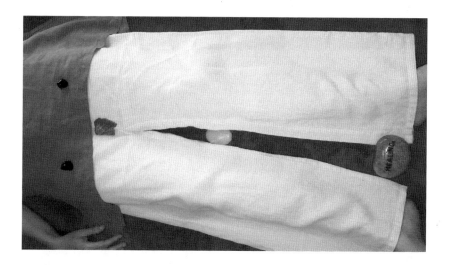

⊙ Larger central stone: smoky quartz, red stone (jasper, red coral)

⊙ Hip joint stones: bloodstone, jasper, red coral, calcite

⊙ Optional between knees if sensing anxiety/fear – rose quartz

◎ Grounding stone between ankles: Denser, darker colored stone such as sodalite, calcite, malachite, darker amethyst. Avoid clear quartz crystal, even if being programmed. Using black stones for grounding (hematite, obsidian) may unbalance the person.

#2 Sacral Chakra

✓ Alleviation of pain and energetic blockages and lower digestion and elimination challenges

✓ Reproductive issues for women

✓ Issues related to how one moves through life, sensuality, quality of relationships, creativity, abundance

✓ Increase intuition and creativity

✓ Strengthen feminine energy in the body

◎ Central stone, preferably rectangle or oblong: carnelian, amethyst, orange calcite

◎ Six to eight smaller stones spaced around it, even distance from central stone: same stones as above (can program clear quartz for substitution on smaller stones)

#3 Solar Plexus Chakra Spread

✓ Healing of pain and energetic blockages in the area

✓ Strengthening key organs (liver, gallbladder, stomach, spleen and also helps diaphragm, pancreas, and upper digestion)

✓ Issues related to power, confidence, assertiveness, self-esteem, advocacy for self and others

✓ Shielding from negative energy and psychic attack

✓ Strengthen masculine energy in the body

◎ Four stones, one placed over key organs of liver, gall bladder, stomach, and spleen

⊙ Yellow stones are sometimes a challenge to locate. Suggest citrine, yellow mookite (jasper), golden calcite for stomach and gall bladder

⊙ For liver and spleen, use stones that support the blood such as amethyst (darker the better), tiger iron, or *small* pieces of bloodstone (on liver), or pyrite

#4 Heart Chakra Spread

✓ Strengthening the lungs, heart and rib cage, upper arms the heart chakra heals and expands in levels

✓ Relief of anxiety and fear

✓ Removal of blockages to manifesting

✓ Ability to give and receive love and nurturing

✓ Living with the heart rather than the toxic ego in charge

⊙ Central stone, preferably round or chunk: jade, emerald, seraphinite, labradorite

⑤ Five smaller stones spaced around it, even distance from central stone. You program clear quartz for substitution on smaller stones if required.

⑤ Avoid fluoride and malachite for the central stone. Their energy is not as stable for this purpose.

Note: If a person has a heart condition, do the spread for the Heart Chakra on the Root Chakra, intentionally sending the energy with your mind to the heart.

#5 Throat Chakra Spread

✓ Releasing blocks to all forms of communication

✓ Strengthening all forms of communication, including self-expression

✓ Increases ability to hear your Guides and your Higher Self

✓ Activates ability to channel

✓ Physical healing of sinus, ear, throat and upper respiratory issues

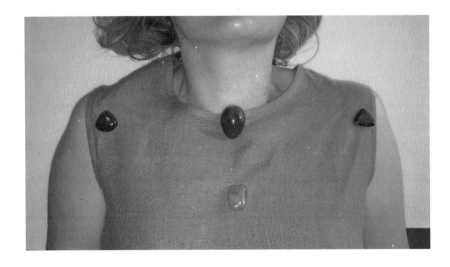

⊚ Central stone is high vibration blue stone. For physical issues, use darker color stones such as lapis lazuli or sodalite. For energy/spiritual activation, use aqua aura or aquamarine

⊚ Three smaller stones such as lapis lazuli, sodalite, fluorite, blue calcite, tourmaline or aquamarine. Place one on each shoulder joint and the third below the larger central stone.

#6 Third Eye and Crown Chakra Spread

As the upper chakras are incredibly sensitive to the use of Crystals with Reiki, caution is suggested. Know that less is more. You must ground the person upon completion of this spread. I suggest following up with the Root Chakra spread. With this spread, your intention must be clear and remain your focus throughout.

✓   Activating Third Eye abilities to see the bigger picture

✓   Increasing your sense of connection with the Divine

✓   Improved auditory receiving of messages from Guides

✓   Expanding and strengthening brain functioning

✓   Healing inner ear issues, especially related to balance and hearing

◎   Nine stones forming a halo at least 1 inch from head

◎   Suggest amethyst though can include some fluorite, chaorite

◎   Note: Only if the client is of a higher vibration, experienced in energy work and well grounded in daily life, then you can place an small additional stone on 3rd Eye for activation of higher vision, such as kunzite, phenacite, and Herkimer diamond. Add grounding stone between feet (see root chakra for information on grounding stones for this spread).

Reiki and Crystals Healing Grids

Crystal Healing Grids are an ancient technique for healing, strengthening, expansion, and manifesting both in the here and now and for distance. To create a grid, you place crystals in an intentional, geometric pattern with a specific intention. Grids are very powerful healing tools on their own, but when charged with and by Reiki, they are a very focused, powerful form of energy work with quite amazing results. The purposes of using Crystal Healing Grids with Reiki are as follows:

- Catalyst and conduit for healing and change

- Maximizes intention when manifesting

- Vehicle to provide ongoing healing without the need for your presence

- Empowers you as a healer by expanding your influence

- Creates a stronger channel of communication with your Guides

- To send healing and support to a present or future event

How to Create and Activate a Grid:

1. You, or your client, defines an intended goal.

2.   You'll need a flat round shape, about the size of a dinner plate. Even a perfect circle cut out of paper will suffice.

3.   Write your intention and place it under the grid chart. If for a particular person, write down their name and intention. Directions for writing an intention follows this section.

4.   Choose stones that both your assessment and intuition advise you are the best fit for this intended healing or request. (Refer to directions for Healing Spreads for Chakras for information on stones that fit each chakra). You need to choose one central stone and 12 smaller stones.

5.   Cleanse and charge the stones with Reiki and add symbols.

6.   Choose a place for your Grid where it will be undisturbed for the prescribed period of activation (as stated in your written intention). If unsure of the period of time, use the Energy-testing technique in this book to determine duration e.g. hours, days, weeks, etc.,

7.   Place the central stone on the grid. Place the 12 smaller stones around the grid's perimeter, similar to the numbers on the face of a clock. Follow your intuition as to which one to place where.

8.   Each day during activation, charge the Grid with Reiki for at least 10 minutes while focusing on the written intention. Think of charging the entire grid and not the individual stones.

9.   When it is time to dismantle the Grid, thank the Guides for their assistance and cleanse the stones. You can discard the intention as it is done!

Writing Intentions for a Reiki and Crystals Healing Grid

Being specific with your intention when activating a healing grid is very important. The clearer you are, the better the Guides and the Reiki and Crystals Frequency can respond and assist with your request.

Writing down the intention gives it form and makes it more concrete and strong. Specifying the amount of time you would like your grid to be active is important. An example is: "Until current healing need is complete."

If you use a grid to help you with a specific event, keep it active until results are achieved. One of the primary reasons for this is so that the activation will continue with or without your physical presence or thinking about the grid.

If you are creating a grid for someone else, have them write the intention. If a person is not physically present or unable to state their intention or give you a clear indication of what they require, follow the directions for distance healing you have learned in a class to gain permission for healing and then develop the intention for them. (If you have not learned this yet, place your focus in your Heart Chakra, connect with their Heart Chakra and intuit if there is an open connection between the two of you. If there is resistance or lack of connection, then a Grid may not be for their highest good).

Create and write your intention in this format if for yourself:

May the Reiki Guides and Ascended Masters bring Heaven and Earth together and activate this healing grid to assist with my intention. My intention is _____ , with this grid remaining active for/ until _____ .

Create and write your intention in this format if for someone else:

May the Reiki Guides and Ascended Masters bring Heaven and Earth together and activate this healing grid to assist _____ with the following intention. The/their intention is _____ _____ , with this grid remaining active for/until _____ .

Part IV

Channeling with Reiki and Crystals

Reiki and Crystals –
Channeling with Fire and Ice

They say that the world is a microcosm of the Universe which is our microcosm. They say that all is energy and that energy is Light. Out of Light energy came sound energy in the original creation. Out of Light and Sound comes the foundation of all that there is. Each object, whether solid, liquid or gas has its own code which is a vibratory frequency. This vibration is created out of Light.

~ from *The Light Shall Set You Free*
Drs. Norma Milanovich and Shirley McCune

We know that crystals have amazing, inherent metaphysical properties as the natural result of the combination of chemical properties from which they were created, their alignment with and infusion of Mother Earth's vibration, and any particular work that has been done with them by forces from higher realms. What you've learned and practiced in the previous sections of this book lays the foundation for channeling and the potential for your expansion with this unique work. You'll receive knowledge and Light Activations while learning to receive insights, directions, revelations, and healing for you and those you assist.

Channeling the Reiki and Crystals Frequency puts you on a platform to receive information guidance and healing from higher sources and other dimensions. This includes your Guides, Ancestral Guides,

Angels, Mother Earth, Elementals and other realms. It also includes rapid expansion of ability to hear your inner wisdom through your Higher Self. The energy and information that you'll receive will feel like it flows from another source.

Reiki and Crystals together are like the metaphysical internet sending emails to you that allow you to search the universal web for what is required. You'll experience:

- Rapid expansion of your vibration

- Strengthening your Reiki and your abilities

- Access to inherent knowledge and programs of the crystals or minerals you use

- Opening as a conduit for information and awareness from other sources

- New insights for healing required and the root cause of issues

- Expansion as a channel for new energies for others, yourself and the planet

To this point, Reiki energies have healed you and raised your vibration to a level so that this ability can activate within you now. Right now the Earth needs Lightworkers with advanced skills to move the planet forward in accordance with the divine plan and cosmic law. Now, you are to experience the process of transforming energy frequencies and patterns of Light into information and energy that resonates with, and can be utilized in the third-dimensional world. This is a form of alchemy and opens your potential further than ever before.

Crystals are powerful tools and allies in this process. People can and do channel without them. As you are now open to their majesty and brilliance married with Reiki, not accessing their knowledge is like being a visually-challenged person without glasses or a hearing-impaired person without hearing aids. Information can still get through, but the details and vividness are compromised.

What is Channeling?

Channeling is the ability to bring information, insights, awareness, connections and energies from other dimensions for use on the Earth.

Each of us is born with etheric antennae that can access energy and information from realms of consciousness not usually seen in the third-dimensional world. Those who can easily receive this way have more of those antennae open for business. Some people have genetic predispositions to this or have soul purposes aligned to being more tuned in naturally. This does not mean that these people are better or make better channelers – it's simply that they are more readily built to do so.

When attuned to Reiki degrees, your vibration strengthens, awakening abilities and opening channels to be such a conduit. The experiences of being attuned and re-attuned to Reiki degrees strengthens and increases your number of 'antennae' to higher knowledge.

The Reiki and Crystals Frequency will open the ability in you more quickly than Reiki alone. This frequency is very Fifth Dimensional in nature, raising your consciousness to a higher realm and anchoring it there for easier access to the Field of all Possibility. So before we begin to open these abilities in you, it is essential to set some intentions and boundaries to what you desire to access. If you think right now "I want it all" then you will be setting yourself up for burnout and fatigue. Respecting your comfort zone and desires are confidence building for you, and honors you as a Lightworker. Go slow with this process, be self-aware of the experience and impact on you. From that, you can define how you wish to embody the role as a channeler of the Reiki and Crystal Frequency.

Top Ten Crystals for Channeling with Reiki

You've learned in this book how commonly-known properties of a crystal can be experienced in a different and always exceptional way with the Reiki and Crystal Frequency. This following list provides you with 10 recommended crystals *in no particular order* for channeling with this powerful Frequency. As you do your own exploring practice, you will find others. Look to those in your collection already. As you read the following Top Ten, be mindful of your kinesthetic experience with them. How does your heart center and your entire body experience each one? These signals are keys from your Guides as to the optimal ones for you right now:

#1 Elestials

From the quartz family, this powerhouse crystal is not often considered pretty, as it appears to be pulled together piecemeal with little consistency in form or design. Know that Elestials are one of the most powerful crystals available on the planet. They are not meant for daily wear. Doing so can weaken the endocrine system.

They're not recommended as your first crystal when opening and learning to channel due to their powerful nature. Just go to Elestials after you've had some practice with channeling – you'll know when the time is right. Always use several grounding stones when working with these beauties. Elestials are great tools for channeling as:

1. Elestials seek and project the highest form of truth.

2. Aligns the head and the heart to work together optimally.

3. Powerful messages from the Ascended Masters and Angels are more easily received.

4. Channeling with Elestials opens your Crown and Third Eye while working with the transpersonal point above your Crown Chakra for the clearest reception.

#2 Golden Healer

My sense is that Golden Healer's time has come to be recognized and utilized to its fullest potential. It will reveal itself to you in waves, almost as if it tests your intention and resolve in living in the light. Golden Healer fills your auric field and that of anyone you assist with high-frequency golden healing light. You are then connected to the Frequency of the Oneness of All in the Fifth Dimension. Your work is transported to a much higher level and surrounded with grace.

Golden Healer is essential with Reiki and Crystals for channeling and healing work as:

1. It aligns your chakras, meridians, and energy pathways, so you are a clear channel to receive.

2. Enables the connection for you with the Christ Consciousness, which is the frequency that Jesus held, demonstrated, and taught to us.

3. Golden Healer keeps integrity in your thoughts, words, and actions as a channel and healer.

#3 Apophyllite

Whenever I meditate with Apophyllite, I experience being surrounded by Angels and their realm. So beautiful and multi-faceted, this graced crystal stimulates a higher vision with the ability to gain new perspective and insights from the angelic realms to your highest self.

Apophyllite holds a perfect representation of the Reiki and Crystal Frequency. As a channeling tool:

1. Apophyllite creates a crystal clear channel to higher knowledge and wisdom without interference or distortion.

2. It incapacitates the ego's ability to influence the messages and insights you receive for yourself or others.

3. Lower-frequency energies are transmuted, healing the recipient and yourself while channeling.

#4 Herkimer Diamond

Herkimer Diamonds chose me early on my journey. After 20 years, they still reveal more and offer new pathways within me. There is a purity and limitlessness to their nature and are essential for every healer. Herkimer Diamonds are second to diamonds on the Mohs Scale of Hardness at 9.5. Acquire those that come from Herkimer, New York. There are others coming on the market from other places, but they do not have the same vibration as original Herkimer Diamonds.

They unwaveringly reveal the depths of who you are to yourself, clearly pointing out the illusions and core beliefs that you hold which you need to move out for soul expansion. For your personal healing and growth, choose them when you desire to excavate yourself, hear your inner truth and embrace the emotional and physical release that can come from this process. You'll be overjoyed with the results!

What is very unique about Herkimer Diamonds is that they can have many physical flaws. These flaws are pure gold for a channeler, so look for a Herkimer at least the size of a quarter and full of internal cracks and rainbows. If you could secure a rare Record Keeper (triangle naturally etched on the side) or an Enhydro (water bubble within), jump at it. Each of these flaws is an opening to higher realms and information, and some hold portals to other dimensions. As channeling tools:

1. Herkimer Diamonds unify your body, mind, emotions, and spiritual self so that you are fully present in both receiving and communicating what you've learned.

2. The connection with Spirit and the Ancestral Guides of the person with whom you are working is bridged.

3. Herkimer Diamonds enables acceptance and understanding for yourself and others, while pulling in the nurturing frequency of the divine feminine.

4. You can excavate yourself fearlessly, holding the mirror up so you can see what no longer serves you.

#5 Stilbite

Though this crystal may be unfamiliar to you, it is time for you to get to know her. An essential in any energy healer's toolbox, it is a necessity for anyone working with Reiki and Crystals. Stilbite heals while infusing the recipient with nurturing energies and opening new creativity and intuitiveness in the body. I often hold Stilbite while sending energy at a distance, trusting that its purity of nature and access to high healing frequencies are optimally transmuting the issue at hand.

Stilbite is an excellent stone for channeling with Reiki and Crystals. It provides an incredibly clear channel to your Guides and those of the person, animal or situation you are assisting. Ancestral Guides and people who have passed over find Stilbite and Reiki provide a great channel for their connection in this dimension. Here are some other key points for Stilbite:

1. Often for a channeler, the Third Eye and Crown centers open too wide, with few filters for what is not helpful. Stilbite prevents this, ensuring a clear and focused channel is available.

2. Channeling with Stilbite also heals the healer or channeled. It nurtures, leaving you reinvigorated and present after the session.

3. Stilbite alleviates fear. It clears the heart field of the channeler and the client, moving out debris and healing the past joyfully.

#6 Kunzite

Each healer gravitates to certain crystals, and Kunzite is one for me. It is ancient stone, which communicates wisdom from the past, insights for the future and information from other realms for optimal use in the here and now. At the same time, it keeps your vibration high while supporting you as a spirit in the flesh.

Kunzite can be named 'the beacon stone.' Once an intention is determined, it lights the path of least resistance for its attainment. It works with the heart field while doing this, enabling access to the realm of all possibility for manifestation. For optimal manifesting, your connections with your Guides and your psychic abilities needs to be clear. I find that when I channel with Reiki and Kunzite, something amazing opens up for both the receiver as well as myself. In the days following the session, the magic begins with synchronicities, gifts and new insights arriving constantly.

She is the Goddess in earthly form. Here are some additional ways to love kunzite:

1. It partners well with any other crystal you may want to use, like a best friend pushing the other along to work at the highest levels possible.

2. Kunzite helps to quiet and subdue the logical mind that can often interfere with the channeling process.

3. The wisdom that comes through divine feminine energies is bridged for you with kunzite. As a channeler, you do not simply want information; you require wise counsel that is always for the highest good.

#7 Titanium Quartz Crystals

As with Aqua Aura found in the Top Ten list earlier in this book, Titanium Quartz is also created by human interference. Clear quartz is coated with the metal titanium and placed in a vacuum chamber. Magic happens!

Most crystals on the Top Ten Channeling list are clear-to-opaque in color. Titanium Quartz is dark green and blue to indigo at its base, with highlights of brilliant colors so that it incorporates the healing vibration of the entire color spectrum. Titanium Quartz is a great crystal for the beginner channeler with Reiki as it's very gentle and opens up your inner physical and energetic channels. It also strengthens your ability to channel as it connects you with higher realms.

It is essential to use a grounding stone with Titanium Quartz as it can move you out of your body. As a channeler, you need to be very present and remain in your body and heart center while receiving. When activating Titanium Quartz and channeling with Reiki and Crystals, know that:

1. Titanium Quartz heals both the channeler and the receiver of the information, especially in the auric field of both people. The aura emits from your body in seven levels that parallel your chakras, and auric healing must occur for chakra strengthening that leads to physical healing.

2. This crystal helps you communicate information with wisdom, compassion, and grace to the receiver. It gives the channeler a very grounded experience while providing insights into your process and needs, even while receiving for others.

3. As you evolve on the path of enlightenment, Titanium Quartz assists you in a very fifth-dimensional way to allow your Soul to usurp the ego and take the lead in your life. You'll receive information and insight about how to allow your Soul to lead.

#8 Phantoms and Inclusions in Quartz Crystals

This category does not refer to one specific crystal, but rather qualities found in quartz crystals: Phantoms and Inclusions. Phantoms are internal layers of cloudiness or an opaque shadow that looks like a ghost or a spirit inside the crystal. Usually white or even green, a Phantom may appear as a streak or a layer, sometimes in a chevron shape. Phantoms readily connect you with spiritual guidance, and help you move quickly into that zone required for channeling. Phantom crystals also provide the energy for evolution, growth, and change.

What's exciting with Phantoms for the channeler is that they often hold information that is hidden or stored, intended to be revealed at the optimal moment to shine light on the shadow side of a situation or issue at hand. Phantom energy illuminates where the truth lies, providing the insight required for the person receiving the information to find their solutions and move forward. What is revealed through them activates an individual's resolve within to put that one foot in front of the other and take those steps forward in life.

Inclusions are another specific form or shape held within a Quartz crystal. Enhydros are water bubbles within a crystal captured at their birth. Inclusions can also be rainbows or cracks and crevices within a crystal that form a particular shape, and may be recognizable such as an angel or dragon. And another form of inclusion is called an occlusion, which is the deposit of another mineral within a crystal. When you find an occlusion, it will maximize the inherent energy and power of the host crystal.

Additional points on channeling with crystals that have Phantoms and Inclusions are:

1. You may want to use a particular crystal with a phantom or an inclusion for a certain person, yet sense that it may not be right. Trust your intuitive knowing, as well as using the Energy-testing directions found earlier in this book to check if it is the optimal one to use.

2. Some of the Phantoms that will come across your path as a channeler will only be for you in times of growth and expansion. Be mindful of those and respect that they are the gift for you.

3. It's really important not to overthink when you're using a Phantom or an Inclusion. Avoid focusing on the shape or the

style that you see inside, or coming to any conclusions about its meaning or purpose.

9 Selenite

Selenite appears on both the Top Ten lists with Reiki and Crystals and this advanced list. The vibration of the family of Selenite most closely matches the vibration of the Fifth Dimension than any other crystal. Selenite can generate, amplify, and ground new energies in the body for healing and expansion, and doesn't require cleansing itself.

Let's focus on her use as a channeling tool. In Merlin's message found earlier in this book, Selenite says that "light consciousness and the breath of life flows through me, through Selenite runs the vibration of the Earth and our healing wisdom and strength." Selenite connects you with Source energy, moving through your Crown and your Heart Chakras. Its beauty knows no bounds, especially with intention. When activating the Reiki and Crystal Frequency with Selenite your consciousness as Channeler moves to higher realms of awareness and energy. Assisted by the Angelic realms, Selenite brings that frequency back for use on the Earth plane.

In the Fifth Dimensional Consciousness Program I teach, we work in-depth with Selenite as it anchors the user as a fifth-dimensional being in the third-dimensional world. Some additional points when channeling with Selenite that are important to know:

1. Ground your energy when using Selenite. Often, I just put the Selenite on the floor by my feet next to a grounding stone rather than holding it in my hand or near my heart. It works without the channeler feeling energetically frazzled afterward.

2. Respect the multi-dimensional power of Selenite. Always be conscious of remaining in your heart center as Selenite can rapidly

open up the Third Eye and Crown Chakras. For a new channeler, it can be a little overwhelming.

3. Selenite is very eager to help. Selenite will call to you, and you'll feel its pull often. Use Selenite with a great discernment, knowing that there are times when you need a different, quieter vibration for channeling or healing than what Selenite provides. Selenite wants to be the life of the party!

#10 Moldavite

It is a naturally formed glass, or tektite, that formed as the result of a meteor hitting the Earth. Moldavite prodded me to include it on this list. There were many times where I questioned whether that should happen, but its wisdom and its need to be here was unwavering.

My hesitancy is in knowing what an incredibly strong frequency it holds, even without Reiki energies. Moldavite requires adjustment to work with it and remain grounded. It's not for every channeler. Once you've aligned as a channeler with the energy of Moldavite and Reiki, it will be a presence moving in and out of your life, so taking the time to build a relationship with it is important.

When activating Moldavite with the Reiki and Crystal Frequency, you will be able to connect with any information, guidance, wisdom, and insights that you or the person that you're assisting requires. It is that powerful, but it can be quite the trip – like a rider on the back of a never-ridden horse. Know that Moldavite will directly connect you with the extraterrestrial realms. If you are a person who is not desiring nor comfortable with that experience, you can choose not to work with Moldavite. Moldavite can keep you out of your body in a way that exhausts you over time. You may find its frequency too strong to have with you while meeting life's requirements through the day. I love working with Moldavite, yet avoid wearing it.

In saying that, for channeling, it is unbelievable. It provides the answer before you even ask the question. It brings with it the energy of transmutation, which is the force that moves the caterpillar to the butterfly. Moldavite when channeling will assist you in pulling through energy and the insights for another, especially if substantial changes or disconnection from toxic energy is required for them. Once you adapt to Moldavite's energy, it will come through a session even when it is not present. Here's some additional information about Moldavite and Reiki with channeling:

1. Being well-grounded throughout your connection with Moldavite is essential. Both you and the person you are assisting will want to have a grounding stone by your feet.

2. Moldavite will move stuck energy, hidden emotions and awaken dormant talents and abilities. Take time to allow whatever is revealed, even if it is emotional, and work with what arises. Avoid making rapid changes as Moldavite is a stone that brings the energy of change with it.

3. Before you begin bringing Moldavite into sessions with others, take a committed period of time to work with it with the Reiki and Crystal Frequency. Journal about your experience. In doing this, Moldavite will become a very powerful teacher and life help-mate for you.

Raise Your Vibration to Prepare for Channeling

When using Reiki and Crystals for channeling for yourself and others, maintaining your high vibration is essential. Creating sacred space is essential. Having a high vibration and creating sacred space includes:

- Being free of distraction, noise and having all *electromagnetic devices off*

- Not being overly fatigued or stressed

- Permitting yourself to release expectations about outcomes

- If channeling for another, ensure that they are settled and grounded. You may want to do some Reiki for them first

- If channeling for yourself, ensure it is not a time where you are anxiously seeking 'the right answers'

- Use only high vibration stones on or near you, as close to the heart chakra level as you feel comfortable

- Keep paper and pen nearby

The next three exercises assist in your preparation. 'Preparing yourself' is always done before channeling. Sharing these exercises with my students has had phenomenal results and opened them in new and exciting ways as Lightworkers. Number One and Two are meditations for you to practice to open your channeling abilities and increase your psychic antennae. Practice them frequently as Light Activations are embedded in them. The third exercise provides the directions to prepare yourself before each channeling session. If you have not yet been attuned to all the symbols listed, use the ones that you have.

Prep #1 Place of Grace

Grace is a state of being. You cannot think your way into it, yet being mindful in daily life is the key. This exercise releases major blockages people carry to living in Grace. This meditation is part of the Fifth Dimensional Consciousness Program I teach and have been guided to share with you here.

To prepare: Sit comfortably in a chair or in a meditation position on a pillow. Comfort is key. This meditation takes 20 to 30 minutes. Hold a gentle, opaque crystal such as rose and smoky quartz, calcite, or amethyst to which you add the Reiki symbols you have. Place a grounding stone (not black) by your feet.

To begin: Breathe deeply and rhythmically with the intention of your breath reaching the floor of your pelvis. You may need to do a few rapid breaths at first to release stress and physical tension. The following directions are written with you looking out from yourself (not looking at yourself).

Directions:

1. Place your attention in your Heart Chakra.

2. Notice (see or feel) in front of you a red picnic blanket. Place any distracting thoughts you may be having on the blanket. See or feel yourself lifting all four corners and tying them together in a bundle.

3. Notice or feel the bundle move to 10 feet or 3 meters behind you. Say to yourself "The past does not exist." Repeat 3 times.

4. Place your hands flat on your Heart Chakra in the center of your chest. Breathe normally and focus your breath to your hands.

5. With your eyes closed:

   a. Notice a point 3 feet (1 meter) in front of your body, and then

   b. Notice a point 3 feet (1 meter) to the right of your right shoulder, and then

   c. Notice a point 3 feet (1metre) behind you, and then

   d. Notice a point 3 feet (1 meter) to the left of your left shoulder.

   e. Starting at the front point and moving to the right, connect these points until a circle is drawn completely around you.

6. With your eyes still closed:

   a. Notice a point 3 feet (1 meter) above your head, and then

b. Again notice the point 3 feet (1 meter) behind you, then

c. Notice a point 3 feet (1 meter) into the Earth directly below your tailbone, then

d. Again notice the point 3 feet (1 meter) in front of you.

e. Starting with the point above your head and moving backward, connect these points until a circle is drawn completely around you.

7. Notice the two circles you have created. How does it feel in the perfect center of these circles?

8. Call on the Divine Feminine to fill the sphere around you that you've created with the two circles. You may call on Mother Mary, Isis, Quan Yin or a female Ascended Master that has pure love meaning for you. Notice what you notice. How does this feel around you? How do you feel with this force around you? What else do you notice in your body? Ask for any anxiety, stress, fear and pain to be dissipated and washed away. Believe that you deserve to have your anxiety, stress, fear and pain washed away. (Allow this to resonate for several minutes).

9. Open to higher frequencies of Love and Light. Allow joy to fill all the spaces in and around you in your bubble (allow this to resonate for several minutes).

☉ Now, what is the name of this place you are sitting in? What shall you name it so you can call it back to you again and again?

⑤ While in your Place of Grace, allow gratitude to move from your heart and fill your body. Allow gratitude to fill the sphere around you. Invite gratitude to become one with your auric field and move with you throughout each day.

10. Know that this Place of Grace is a state of being that is now familiar to you. Every cell in your being is now activated to resonate with the Frequency of Grace. You can call on this place of nurturing and healing and allow the presence of Grace to be at your core each day.

To Finish: Bring your awareness back to this place and time. Focus on your physical form – notice your feet flat on the floor, feel how your body is being supported where you sit. Move your fingers and your toes. Make larger movements with your arms and legs and wiggle your bottom. Take a few deeper breaths and open your eyes when ready. Sit in silence for a few minutes and drink in all that you have experienced.

Prep #2 Meeting Your Channeling Guide

While being attuned through this process to channeling with the Reiki and Crystal Frequency, you receive the gift of a very powerful Guide to assist you. Know that you are opening to a very high vibration process – to translate what is known in the etheric realms for use in our world.

This following meditation activates the arrival of this Guide. While writing this, I sense how big this step you are taking is for your soul purpose, which is actually affecting my ability to write!

To Prepare: Review the following steps. When ready to mediate, commit to 20 to 30 minutes. Place a clear quartz crystal in your hands and a denser colored stone (not black) at your feet. Focus your awareness in your Heart Chakra, guiding it back there whenever it wanders. (You may want to think about who they are or figure out who they are, but it's about feeling them through your heart).

To begin: Take a deep breath in. Do that again. Notice how your feet connect with the Earth. When you are opening to channel, start with the Earth. This process is about allowing the Earth to nurture and support you and keep your Spirit grounded and anchored to the Earth.

Directions:

1. As you breathe in and feel your feet on the Earth, allow roots to come out of the bottom of your feet. Allow the roots to move down, down, down into the Earth, knowing that you will be supported. Notice how your breath goes into your chest and your torso. Breath deeper and deeper into your pelvic bowl.

2. Focus on your Heart Chakra. You may see or connect with the color green, or simply be aware of breathing into your Heart Chakra.

3. While in your Heart Chakra, take your attention to your back, and to the feelings and sensations that you have behind you, for your Guide is standing right behind you right now.

4. Through your Heart Chakra, notice what you notice about their energy. Notice what you notice about their presence, size and stature, age, gender, how they're dressed, or how they look. And even if you don't see pictures visually, notice the sense and feeling that you have while connected with them.

5. Feel the love and the joy that they're bringing in for you. Sit in quiet meditation to connect with their essence, and for their essence to connect with you as well.

To finish: Give a prayer of thanks and record your observations. As you repeat this meditation, you will be given more clarity and information.

Prep #3 Preparing Yourself

This third exercise is to be done prior to your client's arrival. It readies you to receive information and energy. Everyone has a different combination of styles in receiving intuitive information. The three primary ways are visual, auditory or kinesthetic (sensate), with one being dominant and the other two following with varying strength. This is different for everyone, so be aware of how you do it and avoid comparing with others who channel.

Prepare yourself by doing the following for each of your chakras (not the clients'). It is important to place a grounding stone by your feet. You'll see that the purpose for each chakra is given as well as the symbols to use. If you have not been attuned to certain symbols suggested, use those you do have.

In the chart on the next page you'll see three columns. The first refers to a specific chakra, and not all chakra's are included. Next, you'll see the higher purpose for each chakra when channeling with the Reiki and Crystals Frequency. The final column indicates which Reiki symbol for you to place in each of your chakras in preparation for channeling. When you place the symbols in each chakra as indicated, say the name three times before you begin.

Chakra	Function	Symbol & Placement
Crown	Gateway for Source Fuel	Dai Ko Myo
Third Eye	Centre for Higher Vision	Chokurei, Distance
Throat	The Translator	3 Chokurei (Say Chokurei 3 times for each symbol and tap in)
Heart	Centre for Discernment and Clarity	Say Hee Kee
Feet	Centre of Balanced Connection	Chokurei, Usui Dai Ko Myo (on top of each foot)

Channeling for Yourself with Reiki and Crystals

Channeling for yourself means that you are opening to receive information, insight, energy and direction from the Spirit Guides and Ascended Masters present for yourself. It is more challenging to receive accurate information for yourself than for other people when channeling. My observation is that channeling – and especially with the higher vibration of Reiki and Crystals – requires you to perform many functions simultaneously while being aware of how your ego, anxieties, and expectations are trying to get in the way!

When a person self-channels, there is usually a life challenge for which you seek insight. Channeling is about insights and information and how they resonate with you and your decision-making process. It takes practice and self-awareness to remain fully in your Heart Chakra and not to allow thoughts that want definitive answers.

Be clear about your intention for asking while simultaneously releasing all expectation of what will be received. As long as you expect your Guides or Angels or the Ascended Masters to solve a problem for you, you will block the flow and not receive clear information or the strongest flow of energy. Open to receive while believing that you are worthy and deserving of their assistance. By doing this – opening to receive and releasing expectation – the clarity and support you desire will arrive.

You'll be asking these four questions in the process of your self-channeling session:

1. On a physical level, what do I require?

2. On a mental level, what do I require?

3. On an emotional level, what do I require?

4. On a spiritual level, what do I require?

Each of these questions refers to the energy body of each four areas. As you know, when the energy body requires healing, then the actual area (physical, mental, emotional or spiritual) exhibits the problem.

Physical refers to the physiological body and includes the health of structures, systems, cells and nutritional requirements. You are asking for energetic information and direction.

Mental is about your thought processes. As your body believes whatever your brain tells it, you need to strive to have high vibration thoughts. These include releasing self-defeating thinking or patterns of thought that interfere with your energy. (See my book: Core of Self). Also, know that your thought processes are impacted by your physical state of being and vice versa. For this exercise, you are asking about what your processing brain requires.

Emotional is your experience of your feeling self. Emotions are complex and never 'black and white' or logic based. They are a powerful guidance system for living an enlightened life. Emotions can be influenced by the other three aspects (physical, mental, spiritual) and arise from this and past life experiences and perception of events in this lifetime.

Spiritual relates to matters of the Soul both within and outside of your physical body. Messages received will assist you on the path of enlightened living.

To Begin Channeling for Yourself:

1. Choose the crystal you wish to hold while channeling, being mindful of its inherent properties.

2. Place the Reiki Symbols you have in the crystal to ensure that it is cleared and activated.

3. Open your energy body by following the Prep #3 directions found before this section.

4. Sit comfortably with your feet connected to the floor.

5. Draw a Chokurei and Usui Dai Ko Myo on top of each foot. If you have not been attuned to these symbols, simply direct Reiki to your feet.

6. Say the following Prayer of Intent:

    May the Reiki Guides, Masters, Healers and Teachers connect me with the highest resonance and purest stream of consciousness that I can access today. Please provide me with insight and information about _____ . I open to receive.

7. Ask the four questions found on the previous page. To finish, give a prayer of thanks and write down your observations and insights. Allow this information to be in your awareness, without jumping to immediate conclusions or answers. Let direction and the solutions come to you, rather than chase after them.

Channeling for Others

When you provide Reiki treatments for others, you often receive messages and insights for them. The expansion of this ability is part of becoming a Reiki Practitioner. You may already provide readings and channeling as part of your practice, or are guided to do so now. Now, as you've opened to the Reiki and Crystal Frequency, this will increase. Here are some guidelines that will help you with this unique role:

1. Be sure that you've worked through all of the exercises in the previous section on channeling for yourself. Being comfortable with the 'Place of Grace' exercise is essential. To be a clear channel for others, you need to be able to create and maintain shielding for yourself and hold sacred space for the process.

2. Follow the guidelines 'Keys for Healers' found earlier in this book.

3. Sometimes the opportunity to channel for someone arises when not expected. Channeling is a sacred process, so do not proceed unless there is private dedicated time for it. Channeling for someone at a party or when socializing may be fun, but you will not be honoring this sacred process nor be receiving the healing energy and information that the person requires.

4. By designating a time and location to assist someone this way allows both you and Guidance to prepare for the process. You will be able to be grounded, neutral, and your Reiki flow will be primed.

5. Explain to the recipient that you are working with a very high vibratory field with the focus being healing and insights. Let them know that you are only providing for them what is received, emphasizing to trust that it is for the highest good.

6. Know that you are providing information and that it is up to the client to make decisions apart from the session you are providing. It is their life, not yours.

7. Setting time limits is very helpful to the process. This not only provides you with scheduling, but it also helps you manage your energy and not become depleted. You are also letting your Guidance know how long their window of opportunity to work through you is open! It is strongly suggested that you schedule a minimum of an hour of time with someone when you are channeling for them. Breaking the hour into three parts is very effective and works in this way:

    The first fifteen minutes: Connect with the recipient and take down information for your records, having them sign whatever consent form that you use in your practice. During this time, you will ask them about their desires, choose and prepare the crystals to assist you and place your hands on their shoulders for several minutes to connect with their energy.

    The second thirty minutes: You are actively receiving information and energy determined by how you are being directed energetically. Begin by saying this prayer of intent as found in the next section. Stay in your zone of receiving, asking the client to hold their questions or comments to the end. (see next page)

The final fifteen minutes: Finalize your session by sharing information and insights received and closing sacred space.

For the Second Part of the Session:

1. If you haven't done so already, choose the crystal you wish to hold while channeling, being mindful of its inherent properties.

2. Place Reiki symbols in the crystal to ensure that it is cleared and activated.

3. Sit comfortably with your feet connected to the floor. Place a grounding stone (not black) by your feet.

4. Draw a Chokurei and Usui Dai Ko Myo on top of each foot. If you have not been attuned to these symbols, simply beam energy to your feet.

5. As the channeler, follow the directions for symbols to be placed in the chakras from Crown to Root. Visualize doing this as your client is present. All symbols are drawn once and tapped in, except for the throat chakra where the Chokurei is drawn and tapped three times.

6. Say aloud the following Prayer of Intent:

    May the Reiki Guides, Masters, Healers and Teachers connect us with the highest resonance and purest stream of consciousness that we can access today. Please provide us with insight and information about _____ for _____ . We are open to receive.

7. Finalize your session by sharing information and insights received, without providing answers for them. Place your hands on their shoulders, speaking a prayer of thanks and use Reiki symbols to close the sacred space.

And One More Thing...

For nearly 20 years, I've been telling my students "Once you are attuned to Reiki, every other healing or energy modality that you have learned becomes heightened and expanded."

You've found through this book that energy of crystals, stones and minerals is not simply enhanced by Reiki, but a new Frequency is activated. As I write these final words, I feel surrounded by Guides thanking me for my efforts and excited about how these words and energies are putting you more powerfully on your true Soul path.

Use this book as a text for your work, an ongoing tool for your expansion and a place of insights and nurturing as you live an enlightened life. Thank-you.

~ Love and Light, Kathy Glover Scott

With Gratitude and Love

Though the process of writing is rather solitary, I have never felt alone. Thanks to those Earthly helpers along the way: Samantha Smith, Ruth McKlusky, Tegan Scott, France Deschenes, Melissa Hornby, Angela Raphael, Ann Thomas, Geza and Magda Toth, Swapna Gopalan, Suzanne Lesperance, Steven Hicks, Tristan Bane, Mary Willemsen, the staff of Singing Pebble Books in Ottawa and the staff of Friesen Press. Thanks to the myriad of crystal sellers and rock hounds who have patiently answered my questions over the years. Especially grateful to my husband, Craig, and son, Thomas, who have not always understood what I am doing, but have carried a ton of rocks for me anyway! Thanks to the Guides and Ascended Masters for the activations, downloads and trials of initiations in the process of completing this book. Love and Light to you all.

Resource Books

My sense is that the internet came to be so that Lightworkers can connect and share information globally. Most people go to the Web for their information on Crystals, yet often find they don't find the depth or scope of what they need to know. Financially supporting book authors is essential to ensuring that in-depth, proven and professional information remains available as we all expand.

About Kathy Glover Scott M.S.W.

Kathy is one of the most recognized and highest vibration teachers of Energy Work and the Healing Arts in Canada. She is one of four teachers of Reiki to the 21st Degree in North America and specializes in moving Advanced Lightworkers forward through the Fifth and Sixth Dimensional Consciousness Programs. She represents the future of being successful in both work and life as she lives fifth-dimensionally in the third-dimensional world.

Kathy is a member of the International Association of Reiki Professionals. She holds both a Bachelor and Masters Degree in Social Work and is a registered psychotherapist and professional member of the College of Social Work. Kathy is a certified Practitioner of Matrix Energetics.

Her home base is Ottawa, Canada and provides classes online and in other locales. With individual clients in person or via Skype, she combines all of her expertise and 30 years experience to provide root cause release of issues and energy blockages, professional consultations and coaching, light activations, attunements, and channeled messages. Kathy masterfully assists you to live your Soul Purposes with prosperity, joy, healthy relationships and to move through life in a State of Grace.

Seminars and keynote presentations are available in your area. To learn more about her exceptional, professional services and classes visit:

www.KathyGloverScott.com
www.ReikiOttawa.com
f Kathy Glover Scott – Reiki Ottawa
@KathyGloverScot (one t on Scot)

Reiki and Crystals: Activating the Power of Fire and Ice is a Certificate Course!

If this book has opened your eyes to the potential of healing and expansion with the Reiki and Crystal Frequency, the online course will move you even further on your journey and in working with others. The course includes:

- Expansion of concepts and information in this book

- Fifth Dimensional facilitated Light Activations and Attunements

- Guided Meditations lead by Kathy Glover Scott

- Channeled symbols to use with Crystals

- Healing Codes to use with Crystals

- Advanced Channeling Techniques

- Directions for Healing Attunements with Crystals for yourself and others

- Advanced Keys for Healers for working with clients

- Information on setting up your practice, including marketing and promotion

- Question Board with in-depth answers

Certificate upon Completion of Program
Visit: www.ReikiOttawa.com for details!

Core of Self

By: Kathy Glover Scott M.S.W.

Written for Lightworkers, Core of Self teaches you the Head-Heart-Gut Model to staying strong and thrive no matter what comes your way! Only through having a strong inner foundation can you live an energized, enlightened life.

The 'Head' is about being in charge of your thought processes and reteaching the ego mind so that you can live from your Heart Center. As your body believes whatever your brain tells it, to advance energetically, you need to become an observer of your own thoughts and learn tools to shift your thinking and maximize manifesting.

The 'Heart' is about living in a State of Grace through knowing what emotions are all about and clearing fear, sadness, and anger. A no-nonsense approach to knowing what your emotions are really trying to tell you and using it advantageously.

The 'Gut' focuses on expanding your Intuition. You'll learn to move through life each day with this 'superpower' guiding you. Your Core of Self becomes strong and confident as you put the Head, Heart and Gut together.

> "Core of Self provides readers the necessary information they need to find the inner strength to take control of their lives. The Head, Heart, and Gut model is easy to understand and has the power to transform thinking patterns into powerful tools that will allow people to discover their true self through unconditional love, happiness, and abundance."
>
> *Maxime B.*